Joomla! 1.6 First Look

A concise guide to everything that's new in Joomla! 1.6

Eric Tiggeler

BIRMINGHAM - MUMBAI

Joomla! 1.6 First Look

First published: March 2011

Production Reference: 1090311

Published by Packt Publishing Ltd.
32 Lincoln Road
Olton
Birmingham, B27 6PA, UK.

ISBN 978-1-849513-42-5

www.packtpub.com

Cover Image by Duraid (duraidfatouhi@yahoo.com)

Credits

Author
Eric Tiggeler

Reviewers
Eric Brown

Mark Kielar

Rita Lewis

Peter Martin

Oleg Nesterov

Acquisition Editor
Dilip Venkatesh

Development Editor
Roger D'Souza

Technical Editor
Dayan Hyames

Indexers
Tejal Daruwale

Monica Ajmera Mehta

Editorial Team Leader
Aanchal Kumar

Project Team Leader
Ashwin Shetty

Project Coordinator
Michelle Quadros

Proofreader
Aaron Nash

Graphics
Nilesh R. Mohite

Production Coordinator
Melwyn D'sa

Cover Work
Melwyn D'sa

About the Author

Eric Tiggeler is the author of *Joomla! 1.5 Beginner's Guide!* and has written two Dutch Joomla! guides, both of which got excellent reviews. He writes tutorials for several computer magazines and for the Dutch Joomla! community website. Over the last 10 years, Eric has developed numerous websites, big and small, many of them using Joomla!.

Eric is fascinated by the Web as a powerful and creative means of communication; and by revolutionary software such as Joomla!, enabling anybody to create beautiful and user-friendly websites.

On a daily basis, Eric works as a consultant and copywriter at a communication consultancy company affiliated with the Free University of Amsterdam. Over the last few years, he has written more than 10 Dutch books on writing and communication. His passion is making complex things easy to understand.

Eric Tiggeler is married and has two daughters. He lives and works in Hilversum (the Netherlands). On the Web, you'll find him on http://www.schrijfgids.nl (in Dutch) and on http://www.joomm.net (in English).

Any book is a team effort, so I'd like to thank everyone at Packt Publishing for their encouragement and commitment to this project. Thanks also to all reviewers for testing the alpha version of this book and helping me create a thoroughly reliable final release!

About the Reviewers

Eric Brown was born and raised in California. He joined the U.S. Navy at 17 and became a Preventive Medicine Technician. Upon exiting military service, he left the medical field behind and moved to Nebraska and entered college to study art and design, which resulted in a Bachelor's of Science in Graphic Design from Wayne State College in Nebraska. Eric has since branched out by teaching himself (or learning from others) various aspects of HTML, CSS, and PHP as well as a variety of other coding languages and web marketing strategies and tools. He currently owns his own media business located in Manhattan, KS, where he lives with his wife and pets.

Over the years Eric has worked for a local design and development firm in Nebraska on such projects as the Golden Spike Tower website aimed at tourist traffic centered on the Union Pacific's Bailey Yard and with a premier pet industry design and development firm as a project manager. He has also written for such prestigious publications as Trafficology (a purchased print publication on web marketing read by over 80,000 people world-wide), CMSWire.com (a leader in content management news), ReveNews (a highly rated site on various aspects of marketing), and Gadgetell (a well-known gadget news site).

Eric was a reviewer for *Joomla! 1.5 JavaScript jQuery* by Packt Publishing. He has also been involved in other books as well providing editing, image touch-up, and custom hand-drawn maps for *Tagging Along* (a Neville Family retrospective) and editing, layout, cover art, and image touch-up on *My Life and Community* (Biography of Ken Huebner).

I would like to thank all those who have helped to bring my career to this point, but most of all I would like to thank my wife Jaime and my two children, Ariel and Autumn, for all their patience and understanding during the development stages of my career and business.

Mark Kielar brings over 25 years of experience in design, photography, commercial art, analysis, and computing to his understanding of open source content management systems such as Joomla! 1.6. He has applied his expertise in web design and development, writing, and editing to projects for organizations as diverse as the Oakland California Charter Schools and Mark Brand Architecture. Mark currently operates his own web design and content management business, Sparkling Finish, in the San Francisco Bay Area.

I'd like to thank my good friends and Joomla! Mentor Rita Lewis at wordstoweb.net and Mark Brand at Mark Brand Architecture for their support in my work in website design and creation. A special thank you goes out to a special friend, Lynne Wardell, who has supported me for many years in all my endeavors.

Rita Lewis has been creating and managing the content of websites for small businesses and creative organizations for the past 20 years working under the name, Words To Web, Inc. During that time she has created and managed Joomla! sites for independent movies for Shayanne Productions and non-profits such as the Interfaith Community Against Domestic Violence. Rita is a regular blogger on Freelance Switch as well as the author of 15 books on Macintosh computing and the Internet, including titles for O'Reilly & Associates, Peachpit Press, and SAMs. Rita has been awarded by the Computer Book Club and The Society For Technical Communications for her efforts.

Peter Martin has a keen interest in computers, programming, sharing knowledge, and how people (mis)use information technology. He has a Bachelor's degree in Economics (International Marketing Management) and a Master's degree in Mass Communication. He discovered PHP/MySQL in 2003 and Joomla!'s predecessor, Mambo CMS, a year later. Peter has his own business `http://www.db8.nl` (founded in 2005) and he supports companies and organizations with Joomla! and Joomla! extension development.

Peter is actively involved in the Joomla! community where he is a member of the Community Leadership Team and Global Moderator at the Joomla! forum.

His other interests are open source software, Ubuntu Linux, Arduino, music (collecting vinyl records), and art house movies. Peter lives in Nijmegen, The Netherlands.

Oleg Nesterov is a professional web developer. He holds a Master's degree in Mechanics and Mathematics (diploma with honors) from Sumy State University in Ukraine. Since graduation, he has figured out the three main principles for his life: having a mission, loving what you do, and constant self-development. He tries to follow each of these principles in his life and job. That's why he's a web developer.

Oleg runs MindK (`http://www.mindk.com`), a web development company that focuses on producing custom Joomla! extensions, templates, and websites of the highest quality. He is an active member of the Joomla! community and speaker at international Joomla! conferences.

He enjoys sharing his experience with others, teaching people, and creating tools that increase developers' productivity.

You can find more about Oleg on his personal website: `http://onesterov.com`.

www.PacktPub.com

Support files, e-books, discount offers and more

You might want to visit www.PacktPub.com for support files and downloads related to your book.

Did you know that Packt offers e-book versions of every book published, with PDF and e-Pub files available? You can upgrade to the e-book version at www.PacktPub.com and as a print book customer, you are entitled to a discount on the e-book copy. Get in touch with us at service@packtpub.com for more details.

At www.PacktPub.com, you can also read a collection of free technical articles, sign up for a range of free newsletters and receive exclusive discounts and offers on Packt books and e-books.

http://PacktLib.PacktPub.com

Do you need instant solutions to your IT questions? PacktLib is Packt's online digital book library. Here, you can access, read and search across Packt's entire library of books.

Why Subscribe?

- Fully searchable across every book published by Packt
- Copy and paste, print and bookmark content
- On demand and accessible via web browser

Free Access for Packt account holders

If you have an account with Packt at www.PacktPub.com, you can use this to access PacktLib today and view nine entirely free books. Simply use your login credentials for immediate access.

Table of Contents

Preface

Joomla! is one of the most popular open source content management systems. It's powerful, it's relatively easy to learn, and it's freely available, which explains why over the last few years it's become the engine behind millions and millions of websites worldwide. In January 2011, the much awaited version 1.6 was released. Version 1.6 is the third major release since the introduction of Joomla! in 2005.

Joomla! 1.6 is a big step forward, introducing great new features such as a flexible content categorization system (enabling you to organize content in as many categories and subcategories as you want) and a new Access Control Levels system, allowing you to control in great detail what logged in users are allowed to see and do on the site. But there's much more to Joomla! 1.6 — a huge number of improvements in usability and functionality that make it more fun, and even less hassle to create state-of-the-art, user-friendly websites. *Joomla! 1.6 First Look* introduces you to all major new features. It focuses on practical examples and helps you to get the most out of the innovations of this new release.

What this book covers

Chapter 1, Stepping up to Joomla 1.6, introduces you to what's new in Joomla! 1.6. You'll learn what's needed to install the new Joomla! release and to upgrade from the previous version, Joomla! 1.5.

Chapter 2, Exploring your Enhanced Workspace, shows you what's changed in the Joomla! backend interface: a new design, new screens, changes in menus and toolbars. You'll learn the practical effect this has on creating and maintaining sites with Joomla!.

Chapter 3, Organizing and Managing Content, covers key changes in Joomla! 1.6 that affect organizing, adding, and editing articles. You'll learn the benefits of using the new system to organize content and you'll learn to use some powerful new ways to present content on your site.

Chapter 4, Managing Menus and Menu Modules, covers enhancements in the way you work with menus and menu modules. Joomla! 1.6 not only makes it easier to manage menu contents and the menu modules, there are also new menu item types available.

Chapter 5, Managing Site Users with Access Control, introduces you to one of the biggest changes in Joomla! 1.6 — the all-new Access Control Levels system. You'll learn how to use this complex system in a practical and efficient way and to control which users are permitted to view and manage content on your site.

Chapter 6, New Flexibility in Using Templates, explains what's new in selecting, using, and editing templates. You'll learn all about a new feature called Template Styles and about the great set of brand new templates that come with Joomla! 1.6.

Chapter 7, Unleashing the New Power of Extensions, focuses on using and maintaining extensions in Joomla! 1.6. The extensions screen has been overhauled, installed extensions can be updated automatically, and some great new modules have been added to the Joomla! default package.

Chapter 8, SEO Improvements, covers the new features for Search Engine Optimization (SEO). In this chapter, you'll find out in what respects Joomla! has become more SEO-friendly and you'll learn more about the techniques you can use to help search engines to find and rank important content on your site.

What you need for this book

To be able to follow along and try out the new features of Joomla! 1.6 for yourself, you need to have Joomla! 1.6 (and the sample data that come with it) installed on your computer or a web server. In *Chapter 1*, you'll find some useful information on installing Joomla! and the server requirements for Joomla! 1.6.

Who this book is for

Joomla! 1.6 First Look is targeted at existing Joomla! users and developers. If you've some experience in using Joomla! 1.5, you're probably curious to find out what's new and how the improvements can help you to create better websites with less effort. You don't want to dive into the basics of Joomla, but you do want to learn about the main new features and try them out for yourself. This book helps you with clear step-by-step instructions, well illustrated with screenshots.

Conventions

In this book, you will find a number of styles of text that distinguish between different kinds of information. Here are some examples of these styles, and an explanation of their meaning.

Code words in text are shown as follows: "Moreover, all heading elements—previously styled with proprietary Joomla! style names, such as contentheading—are now outputted according to web standards, using the H1 (Heading 1) style for the main title, H2 for secondary titles, and so forth."

A block of code is set as follows:

```
<li> id="current" class="active item435">
  <a class="customstyle"
    ref="/index.php?option=com_content&amp;view=featured&amp;
    Itemid=435">Home
  </a>
</li>
```

When we wish to draw your attention to a particular part of a code block, the relevant lines or items are set in bold:

```
<li> id="current" class="active item435">
  <a class="customstyle"
    ref="/index.php?option=com_content&amp;view=featured&amp;
    Itemid=435">Home
  </a>
</li>
```

New terms and **important words** are shown in bold. Words that you see on the screen, in menus or dialog boxes for example, appear in the text like this: "Go to **Menu Manager | Menus** and click on the **Main Menu** name in the **Title** column".

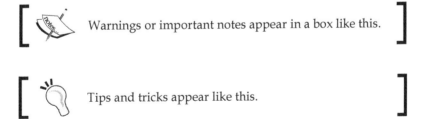

Warnings or important notes appear in a box like this.

Tips and tricks appear like this.

Reader feedback

Feedback from our readers is always welcome. Let us know what you think about this book—what you liked or may have disliked. Reader feedback is important for us to develop titles that you really get the most out of.

To send us general feedback, simply send an e-mail to feedback@packtpub.com, and mention the book title via the subject of your message.

If there is a book that you need and would like to see us publish, please send us a note in the **SUGGEST A TITLE** form on www.packtpub.com or e-mail suggest@packtpub.com.

If there is a topic that you have expertise in and you are interested in either writing or contributing to a book, see our author guide on www.packtpub.com/authors.

Customer support

Now that you are the proud owner of a Packt book, we have a number of things to help you to get the most from your purchase.

Errata

Although we have taken every care to ensure the accuracy of our content, mistakes do happen. If you find a mistake in one of our books—maybe a mistake in the text or the code—we would be grateful if you would report this to us. By doing so, you can save other readers from frustration and help us improve subsequent versions of this book. If you find any errata, please report them by visiting http://www.packtpub.com/support, selecting your book, clicking on the **errata submission form** link, and entering the details of your errata. Once your errata are verified, your submission will be accepted and the errata will be uploaded on our website, or added to any list of existing errata, under the Errata section of that title. Any existing errata can be viewed by selecting your title from http://www.packtpub.com/support.

Piracy

Piracy of copyright material on the Internet is an ongoing problem across all media. At Packt, we take the protection of our copyright and licenses very seriously. If you come across any illegal copies of our works, in any form, on the Internet, please provide us with the location address or website name immediately so that we can pursue a remedy.

Please contact us at copyright@packtpub.com with a link to the suspected pirated material.

We appreciate your help in protecting our authors, and our ability to bring you valuable content.

Questions

You can contact us at questions@packtpub.com if you are having a problem with any aspect of the book, and we will do our best to address it.

Stepping Up to Joomla! 1.6

The Joomla! development team has worked for several years on the latest release, Joomla! 1.6. This may seem like a lot of time, but it's definitely been worth the wait. Important new features have been added, previous limitations have been dealt with, and many improvements have been added. All in all, the Joomla! CMS is fully up-to-date again. It's more powerful, more user friendly, and more fun to work with.

In this chapter, you'll learn what to consider when upgrading from Joomla! 1.5 to Joomla! 1.6 and you'll get acquainted with the main new features and enhancements.

Upgrading from 1.5

If you've installed Joomla! 1.5 before, installing the new version will seem very familiar. The installation process—using the Joomla! installation wizard—has remained unchanged. However, before you start installing Joomla!, make sure that your web hosting account meets the following list of server requirements for Joomla! 1.6.

To enable you to run a Joomla! 1.6 powered website, your web hosting account should support:

- *PHP 5.2 or higher.* PHP is the scripting language that Joomla! is written in.
- *MySQL 5.0.4 or higher.* The MySQL database is where Joomla! stores its data (the contents of your site).

The other system requirements have remained the same since the 1.5 release:

- *Apache 1.3.x or higher.* Apache is the web server software that processes the PHP instructions for how to pull in contents from the database and display a web page.
- *XML and Zlib support.* Your host's PHP installation should support XML and Zlib functionality.

If you don't have a web hosting account yet, it pays to be picky. Although you shouldn't have problems finding a suitable web host, don't just go for any budget hosting service. It's best to have a hosting account allowing you to change certain server settings yourself (typically by editing either a special file named .htaccess or by permission to add a php.ini file with these settings to your account). This will ensure that you can optimize server settings and successfully run Joomla! 1.6 even when your site, your site traffic, and your requirements may change. Examples of good web hosting services for Joomla! are Siteground.com, BlueHost.com, InMotionHosting.com, or Rochen.com.

You can find detailed server requirements at the official Joomla! help site: http://help.joomla.org/content/view/1938/310/.

Joomla! 1.5 extension compatibility

Joomla! 1.5 featured a special legacy mode to maintain downward compatibility with extensions that were written for Joomla! 1.0. Joomla! 1.6 doesn't have such a compatibility mode. This means that all extensions are now required to be "Joomla! 1.6 native". As most extensions developed for Joomla! 1.5 won't run on Joomla! 1.6, extension developers will have to revise their code for the new release.

To check if your favourite 1.5 extensions are already compatible with Joomla! 1.6, go to the Joomla! Extensions Directory (http://extensions.joomla.org). Extensions for 1.6 are marked with a special compatibility label.

Changes for templates

Templates created for version 1.5 can't be used in Joomla! 1.6. The new release uses clean, semantic HTML code, without using tables for layout purposes. This is good news, as template developers are no longer required to add so-called template overrides in order to achieve a semantic design. However, it is one of the reasons that developers will have to upgrade their existing code to move a 1.5 template to version 1.6.

You shouldn't have any trouble finding a suitable template for a 1.6 site. New and updated templates are becoming available every day.

In this book, we won't go into the the technicalities of upgrading template code. If you want to know more, go to `http://www.prothemer.com/blog/tips-and-tricks/7-tips-to-help-convert-your-joomla-1-5-template-to-joomla-1-6/`.

When should you move to 1.6?

If you've got a site running on 1.5 and the extensions you are using haven't been updated to 1.6 compatibility, do not upgrade your production site to Joomla! 1.6. But, you can create a testbed and install 1.6 and get acquainted with the new features. Move to 1.6 when you've made sure that Joomla! 1.6 is stable, all desired features work as they should, and all necessary extensions and templates are available.

Migrating content from Joomla! 1.5

Joomla! 1.6 doesn't contain any functionality to upgrade content developed for a 1.5 powered website to a 1.6 site. The main reason behind this is that the structure of the content database has changed substantially due to some of the feature improvements in 1.6, such as the replacement of the old content organization system (using sections and categories) with a new and more flexible system of unlimited nested categories. You'll read more about that change in the *Working with content* section later in this chapter.

Migrating to 1.6 probably won't pose a problem if you have a small site or if you plan a complete overhaul of your existing website. Switching to the new release can present an opportunity to update both your website and its content. You can copy content manually, pasting existing article text into the article editor of the new Joomla! 1.6 installation.

Upgrading automatically

What can you do if you want to keep all your existing content and the existing structure of your website when upgrading to Joomla! 1.6? Matias Aquirre of Matware has developed a component called jUpgrade that will move your entire site, including its database, from 1.5 to 1.6 automatically. At the time of writing, this component is still under development. To learn more, go to `http://extensions.Joomla.org/extensions/migration-a-conversion/Joomla!-migration/11658`.

What's new? A quick overview

You probably want to get your hands dirty and start right away building a website using this new Joomla! release. Don't worry, we'll get to that in the next chapters. For this chapter, however, let's take it easy. Lean back comfortably and enjoy a guided tour to all that's new in Joomla! 1.6.

There are hundreds of changes in Joomla! 1.6. Some are invisible; these are technical improvements making the Joomla! engine more efficient, doing a better job at powering your website, and making it better optimized with search engines. Other changes are visible improvements to the user interface that make it more intuitive to use. In this section, we'll cover four main fields of improvements: usability, working with content, user access, extensions and templates.

1 - Usability enhancements

Joomla! has been a very powerful tool from its earliest days. However, it didn't always make it easy on its users to unleash all that power. Joomla! users had to get used to jumping around from menu to menu in the backend administration area to perform simple tasks, such as editing a menu item. In version 1.6, the backend user interface (the administration area) is tidied up and simpler to use.

A friendlier interface

At first sight, Joomla!'s restyled and rearranged backend administration area may not seem really different from the 1.5 version . Here's what the new version looks like:

One of the usability improvements that will save you many unnecessary clicks is the introduction of tabbed buttons in many backend screens, allowing you to switch quickly to another screen to perform related tasks.

The screenshot below, for example, shows three tabs that are displayed in the **Article Manager**. When managing articles, these allow you to jump from the **Articles** screen to the **Categories** screen, where you can add or edit article categories, or to the **Featured Articles** screen, where you can assign articles to the homepage:

The administration area layout has been further updated allowing easier access to those features that you use regularly. For example, a new **Users** menu has been added to the top menu that gives you access to enhanced users, groups, and permissions tools (called Access Control Levels or ACL). This menu lets you add users, and define what they can and cannot see or do on the frontend and backend. The **Users** menu is where you set all Access Control Levels (see the *New ways to manage user access* section later on in this chapter).

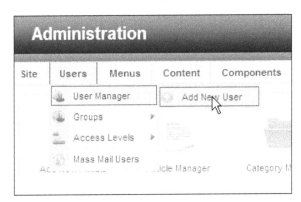

The great new time-saving toolbar

In 1.6, the toolbar in the Administration area contains new options—each of them great time-savers. As an example, here's what the toolbar buttons look like when you're editing an article:

One example of a clever addition is the **Save & New** button. This allows you to quickly create a series of articles one after another without having to close the **New Article** screen.

> In the course of this book, you'll learn more about changes in the way you'll work in the Joomla! 1.6 backend. In *Chapter 2*, we'll focus specifically on all that's new in the administration area interface.

2 - Working with content

The main thing that a content management system should help you in doing is of course to publish content and to manage existing content with minimal effort. In this respect also, Joomla! 1.6 makes some significant steps forward.

The endless joy of unlimited categories

A major innovation is that Joomla! 1.6 allows you to organize content exactly as you want. Up to Joomla! 1.5, you could only classify your content in three levels: sections would contain categories, and categories would hold articles.

Section	Category	Article
Photography	> Camera Reviews	> Pentax kX review

Although this didn't pose problems for most sites, it was nevertheless a strange restriction. That's why Joomla! 1.6 introduces a more flexible system of classification. Categories can now hold an unlimited number of subcategories. This means that you can have a hierarchy like this:

Category	2nd level category	3rd level category	4th level category	5th level category	Article
Photography	> Reviews	> Cameras	> SLR Cameras	> Pentax	> Pentax kX review

A category can hold as many subcategories as you need. This concept is called "unlimited nested categories". In most cases you won't need more than two or three subcategories, but if you do, there's nothing to stop you.

You can check the content category hierarchy in the **Category Manager**. Child categories are displayed indented, with small gray lines indicating the sublevel:

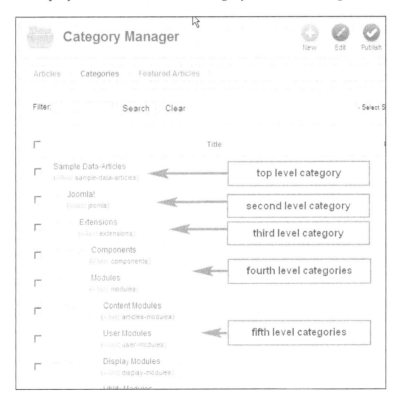

The above screenshot shows the nested categories contained in the sample data that comes with Joomla! 1.6. As you can see, all article content is stored in subcategories of the main category **Sample Data-Articles**.

Displaying the Category Structure on the frontend

You can also have a list of (nested) categories displayed on the website itself as shown in the screenshot below. In Joomla! 1.6, there's a new Menu Item Type available called **List All Categories**. Using this new Menu Item Type you can display an overview of (links to) all site categories. See *Chapter 3, New category view # 1:* **List All Categories** to find out more about the possibilities of this Menu Item Type.

On the next page, you can see an example of the output of the List All Categories Menu Item Type as it is used in the sample site that comes with Joomla! 1.6.

Menu Module

Menus provide your site with structure and help your visitors navigate your site. Although they are all based on the same menu module, the variety of ways menus are used in the sample data show how flexible this module is

A menu can range from extremely simple (for example the top menu or the menu for the Australian Parks sample site) to extremely complex (for example the About Joomla! menu with its many levels). They can also be used for other types of presentation such as the site map linked from the 'This Site' menu

Templates

 Templates give your site its look and feel. They determine layout, colors, type faces, graphics and other aspects of design that make your site unique. Your installation of Joomla comes prepackaged with four templates

Plugins

Plugins are small task oriented extensions that enhance the Joomla! framework. Some are associated with particular extensions and others, such as editors, are used across all of Joomla! Most beginning users do not need to change any of the plugins that install with Joomla!

Park Site

Park Blog

Here is where I will blog all about the parks of Australia

You can make a blog on your website by creating a category to write you blog posts in (this one is called Park Blog). Each blog post will be an article in that category. If you make a category blog menu link with 1 column it will look like this page, if you display the category description (this part) displayed.

To enhance your blog you may want to add extensions for comments, interacting with social network sites, tagging, and keeping in contact with your readers. You will also enable the syndication that is included in Joomla! (in the Integration Options set Show Feed Link to Show an make sure to display the syndication module on the page).

Photo Gallery

These are my photos from parks I have visited (I didn't take them, they are all from Wikimedia Commons)

This shows you how to make a simple image gallery using articles in com_content.

In each article put a thumbnail image before a "readmore" and the fiull size image after it. Set the article to Show Intro Text: Hide.

Animals

Scenery

Fruit Shop Site

Growers

We search the whole countryside for the best fruit growers

You can let each supplier have a page that he or she can edit. To see this in action you will need to create users who are suppliers and assign them as authors to the suppliers articles.

Powered by Joomla!

No more fiddling with menus

Adding menus and editing menus is something you'll do quite often in any CMS. In Joomla! 1.5, this basic functionality sometimes required many steps, clicking back and forth from the Menu Manager to the Module Manager. In 1.6, the **Menu Manager** now contains links to both the menu contents (the menu items themselves) and menu settings (the menu *module details*):

Moreover, when you add a menu link, you're now presented with a new list of clearly understandable Menu Item Types. For example, the Menu Item Type that was previously called **Article Layout** has been renamed to **Single Article**—which anyone new to Joomla! is much more likely to understand:

In the rest of this book, you'll learn more about the new ways of working with content. *Chapter 3* focuses on organizing content. In *Chapter 4*, we'll cover using menus and menu modules.

3 - New ways to manage user access

A major change in Joomla! 1.6 is the new Access Control Levels (ACL) system. It gives site administrators fine-grained control over what registered users can see and do on the website. Site members may have exclusive group access to special content and members of the editorial team may be allowed to access the backend and perform site management actions (such as creating or editing articles).

Joomla! 1.5 featured a basic ACL system: administrators could classify users into a limited number of fixed user groups with predefined rights. In Joomla! 1.6, there are no limits to the permissions system. You can create as many user groups as you like and control the rights of users in detail. In short, you can add users, assign them to custom groups, and define what these user groups are allowed to see and do both on the frontend and backend of the site.

You can set permissions on different levels: on a site-wide level, on the level of components, right down to the level of individual articles or modules. The site-wide permissions are set in the **Global Configuration** Permissions screen:

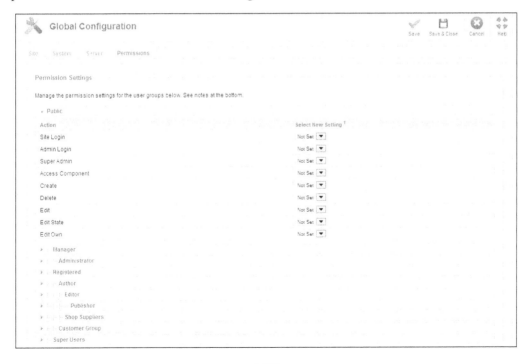

The new ACL system may be very powerful, but it can also be quite complex. You need to carefully plan how you want to set it up. But it can be fun too—it's really cool to be able to specifically control which pages different registered site user groups can see or edit. You'll see examples of this later on in this book.

Do you want it simple? Keep it simple

Of course, you don't have to use ACL when running a Joomla! site. If you're fine with the basic levels of user access that were present in 1.5, you can still use these. The 1.5 ACL levels are still the default configuration—it's just that you can now infinitely extend this system if you need that kind of control.

 In *Chapter 5*, you'll learn more about managing site users with the new Access Control Levels system.

4 - Working with extensions and templates

The availability of numerous high-quality third-party extensions and templates is probably one of the main reasons why Joomla! is one of the most popular CMSes. In Joomla! 1.6, the developers have made it easier to update extensions and they have made applying templates much more flexible.

Updating extensions? Just lean back

Using extensions is great—but there's also a weak point to relying on third party functionality. How do you keep track of updates for all the extensions you're running? In previous versions of Joomla!, you'd have to keep an eye on the Joomla! Extensions Database or the developers sites to see if updates were available. In real life, the difficulty of keeping track of upgrades has meant that many Joomla! sites are running with outdated add-ons, which cause security vulnerabilities and many other problems.

This is where Joomla! 1.6's new **Extension Manager** Update functionality comes to the rescue. With one click, you can search for updates for all installed extensions. If updates are available, you can install them immediately:

Templating to your taste

A strong point of Joomla! has remained: Joomla!'s intuitive template system enables site designers to customize the look and feel of their sites in just a few clicks, by swapping out the current template (and then rearranging module contents to fit the new template).

In Joomla! 1.6, it's easier to apply different templates to customize the looks of specific sections of the site: for example, if the visitor clicks on the News link on your site, another template can be applied, changing the looks of the site to fit that particular section.

Another new feature in this Joomla! release are Template Styles. Styles are combinations of template options, such as the template color scheme. Even if you apply just one template to the entire site, you can still select different template settings for specific site sections. One example of this is that you can have the home page of your site to display with a "green" color scheme (the first template style) and the other pages in the "blue" color scheme (the second template style):

 In *Chapter 6*, you'll learn more about using templates and template styles in Joomla! 1.6. *Chapter 7* gives an overview of all that's new in working with extensions.

SEO improvements

Joomla! 1.6 offers some new features to optimize your site for search engines. It's easier, for example, to apply metadata to specific parts of the site. More importantly, you can now restore broken links to your site by using the new **Redirect Manager**.

This component (working in conjunction with the new Redirect plugin) keeps track of any "page not found" errors that occur when visitors are trying to visit pages that have been removed or deleted. Using the **Redirect Manager** component, you redirect future visitors to the appropriate new URLs.

This feature can be quite useful for people visiting your site through outdated links, as they won't just hit a dead-end error page any more. Moreover, search engine spiders can now keep track of valuable content, even after it has been moved to a new location.

[In *Chapter 8*, you'll read more about SEO improvements in Joomla! 1.6.]

Summary

In this quick tour, we've only just touched upon some major changes in Joomla! 1.6. Let's summarize:

- The server requirements of Joomla! 1.6 have been upgraded. Before you install Joomla! 1.6, check with your web host if your hosting account meets the new requirements.

- Currently, Joomla! 1.6 doesn't contain any functionality to upgrade content developed for a 1.5 powered website to a 1.6 site. You'll have to copy articles manually or use a dedicated content migration extension, once it becomes available.

- Joomla!'s rearranged backend interface is aimed at making it easier and faster to perform administrative tasks, skipping unnecessary steps. Menus have been rearranged, tabs and toolbar buttons have been added or renamed.

- You can now organize content into as many categories as you want. The concept of unlimited nested categories is easier to grasp than the rigid old three level system.

- A major change in Joomla! 1.6 is the new Access Control Levels (ACL) system. It gives site administrators fine-grained control over what registered users can see and do on the website.

- The new **Extension Manager** Update functionality automates the process of keeping all installed extensions up-to-date.

- To adjust templates to your taste, you can now set template 'styles'. Styles are combinations of template settings that you can use to give different parts of the site their own distinctive colors or layout.

- The **Redirect Manager** helps you to automatically point visitors who visit your site through outdated links to updated URLs.

In the course of this book, you'll get to know all these enhanced features and try out how they'll benefit you when building your own site. In the next chapter, we'll focus on the new Joomla! 1.6 workspace. You'll learn how to get the most out of the new features of the revamped administration area.

2
Exploring your Enhanced Workspace

Joomla! has been a very powerful tool from its earliest days. However, the place where you control all that content managing power — the backend administration area — hasn't always been particularly user-friendly. The menu arrangement would sometimes force you to switch back and forth between administration screens to perform simple tasks. For example, if you needed to change an item on one of the site menus, you had to open the menu and then the associated menu module to affect the revision — often repeatedly.

In Joomla! 1.6, the administration area has been redesigned — but the real changes are more than skin deep. All kinds of little usability improvements help you to get things done more efficiently. Let's find out what the main improvements are:

- Before you start: choosing a safe username
- Changes in the backend interface
- Top five time-saving features
- New ways to trash and delete items
- Changing the looks of the backend

Before you start: choosing a safe root user's name

Before we have a look at the backend interface, let's focus for a while on an issue concerning site security — it's about your personal *keys* to the site.

In any CMS, it's vitally important to guard any "doors" through which hackers can grab hold of your site. In Joomla! 1.5, the door to the backend of the site wasn't closed securely due to the system habit of naming the root user (the Super Administrator) "admin" during the installation process. If you didn't change the name "admin" later on, hackers only needed to guess your password to be able to log in to your site.

Joomla! 1.6 rectifies this flaw by letting you enter an Admin Username during the installation process. In previous versions, you could only change this name after installation—and many site administrators apparently didn't bother.

You can now change the root user's name during the installation process (see Step 6, Configuration in the screenshot below). In the **Main Configuration** screen you can enter a specific **Admin Username**, replacing the default value (which is still "admin"). In the **Admin Username field**, enter a name that isn't easy to guess:

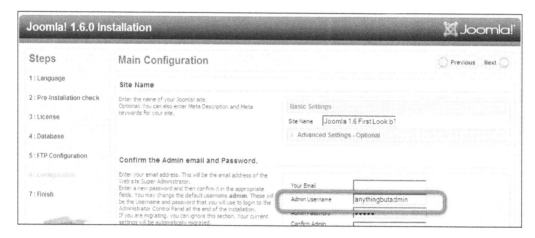

Root user, Super Administrator, Super User, Admin: what's the difference?

When you install Joomla!, there's always one root user, allowed to do anything in the administration area. In Joomla! 1.5, this root user was called Super Administrator. In Joomla! 1.6, this name has been changed to Super User — although this isn't used consistently. In the above screenshot, you can see that you enter the Super User's name in the **Admin Username** field. Just keep in mind that the "Admin" in this case is the same as the root user or Super User.

Another point to note is that the root user is always a Super User — but there can be more Super Users who aren't root users. The root user is a unique Super User who can assign new users to the Super User group. But there's always just one root user created when installing Joomla! Only this root user can change another Super User's details. (You can always identify the root user in the User Manager by his fixed ID number, which in Joomla! 1.6 is always 42).

Changing the root user's name after installation

If you've already completed the installation of Joomla! 1.6 and you haven't chosen a unique **Admin Username** for the root user, you can still do this afterwards. The steps involved have changed a little since Joomla! 1.5, as the **User Manager** has a new location in the backend.

To change any user's login data, go to the backend administration interface. (You'll know the drill if you're familiar with Joomla! If not, see the *Logging in to the backend* section below).

1. Go to **Users | User Manager**.

2. To change the root user's details, in the **Name** column, click on **Super User**:

Clicking on the **Super User** name will take you to the **Edit Profile** screen.

3. In the **Edit Profile** screen, you'll find the **Login Name** in the **Account Details** section. Change this from **admin** to any other name:

4. Click on the **Save & Close** button to save changes.

From now on, you can log in to the backend administration area using the new **Login Name**. Don't let it confuse you: what's called **Login Name** in the **Edit User** screen, is called **User Name** in the login screen for the backend — but it's the same thing.

Logging in to the backend

Now it's time to enter the backend of your site and get to know the new administration interface. To do this, log in to the backend of the site with your admin name and password. Although the entrance page has been redesigned, the login process hasn't changed since 1.5: just navigate your browser to the web address where you've installed Joomla! (such as `www.example.com`) and enter your credentials in the resulting screen:

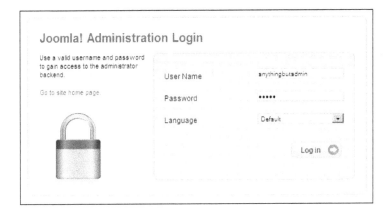

Click on the **Log in** button to enter.

What's changed in the backend?

Let's hear a drumroll for the stylish new Joomla! backend interface! To be honest, the design hasn't changed in any revolutionary way since Joomla! 1.5 (or 1.0, for that matter). However, it has definitely been refined. Here's what the administration area looks like:

To refresh your memory, here's the old 1.5 interface:

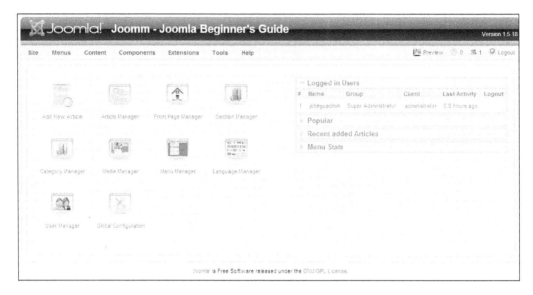

Colors and icons have changed in the new Joomla! 1.6 backend interface, using a new administration template called Bluestork. This gives the interface a pleasing and more modern look. Later in this chapter, you'll find out how you can customize this new template to suit your needs.

But more importantly, menus have been changed and reorganized to make them more logical and easier to use. Let's have a quick look at the three most notable interface changes.

What's gone: no more sections

Instead of both a **Section Manager** and a **Category Manager**, there's now just a **Category Manager**. You can forget the concept of sections altogether: the developers have re-designed how Joomla! organizes content to allow multi-level categories in the place of the rigid Section/Category system. You'll read more this in *Chapter 3* on organizing content in Joomla! 1.6.

What's been added: the Users menu

The **Users** menu has been upgraded from a humble submenu position to one of the main choices offered in the backend control panel as shown in the screenshot below. This change has to do with Joomla!'s enhanced Access Control Levels system, which allows you to manage users, user groups, and their access levels, in great detail. We'll look into this in *Chapter 5*.

What's been moved: some tools and odds and ends

Now where have the Tools gone? The **Tools** menu from Joomla! 1.5 has disappeared. To aid your memory, the old 1.5 **Tools** menu is shown below:

Seen it? Now you can forget it! The Joomla! developers decided to move the contents of the **Tools** menu to menus where they can be found more easily.

The **Global Check-in**, **Clean Cache**, and **Expired Cache** menu items have moved to the **Site | Site Maintenance** submenu as shown in the screenshot below. This makes much more sense, as that is exactly what these options are all about: maintaining your site.

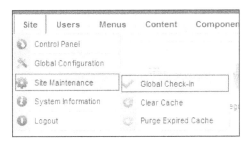

The functionality of these items hasn't changed: the **Global Check-in** option unlocks all items (such as articles) that are currently marked as checked out ("in use") across the whole site. Clearing the cache allows you to delete temporary files that Joomla! creates to improve the performance of your site. This will cause Joomla! to create new copies of these files.

The other options from the old **Tools** menu (**Read Messages**, **Write Messages**, **Mass Mail**) can now be accessed through the new **Users | Mass Mail Users** submenu:

The Mass Mail functionality itself hasn't changed. It's a basic feature, enabling you to send private messages to other users, for example, about site maintenance issues.

User Settings and Media Settings have been moved

In Joomla! 1.5, the **Global Configuration | System** screen would give you access to User Settings and Media Settings. You would look here if you wanted to turn on or off user registration, or revise how images are stored and managed on your site. The Joomla! 1.5 screen is shown below:

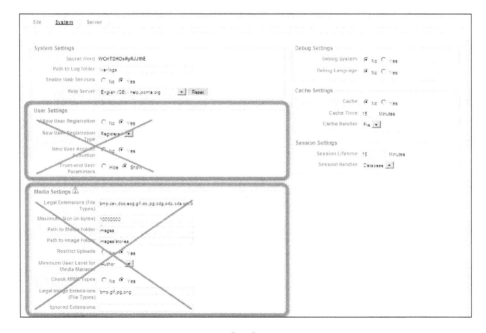

In Joomla! 1.6, you won't find these settings in the **System** screen anymore.

To access the **User Settings** in Joomla! 1.6, go to **Users | User Manager**. Click on the **Options** button and you'll be presented with a pop-up window to manage how and whether users can register on the site:

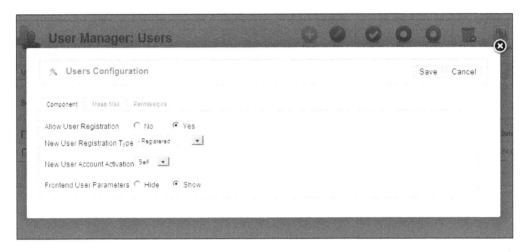

To access the **Media Manager** options, go to **Content | Media Manager** and click on the **Options** button in the toolbar. You're presented with a pop up window that lets you define how images are managed on the site:

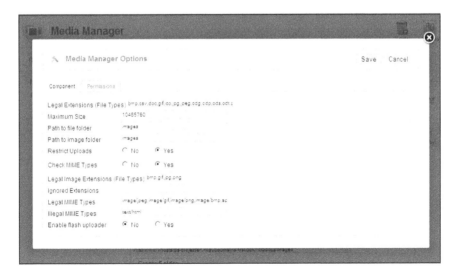

What's the use of the new User Permissions tab?

When browsing the **Global Configuration** screen, you'll notice that there's a new tab called **Permissions**. It's where you set all site-wide user permissions. You'll learn more about this in *Chapter 5* which is about Access Control Levels.

Five great new time-saving features

In the previous chapter, you've already had a sneak peak at the improvements in the Joomla! backend. Apart from a few new toolbar buttons, there are many additional timesavers hidden in the redesigned administration area. Let's find out what they are and how they can help you when you set up and manage your site.

Timesaver # 1: going home in one click

One of the neat little changes in the backend interface, allowing you to work faster: there's a sort of "Home" button now. Just click on the word **Administration** in the top bar. In previous versions of Joomla!, the text here was static. Now it's a hyperlink that takes you back to the backend 'home page', allowing you to jump quickly to the main control panel from any backend location:

Timesaver # 2: adding new items in one click

An extra menu level has been added to Joomla!'s menu interface. Some of the drop-down menu items feature second level ("fly-out") menu items. One example is shown below:

To see for yourself how this works, navigate to **Content | Category Manager** – but *don't* click on the **Category Manager** menu option itself. When the mouse hovers over the **Category Manager** menu item, a new second-level menu item will appear: **Add New Category**. Click on this menu item. This way, you get to the **Category Manager**: **Add New Category** screen in just one step. This saves you the trouble of first opening the **Article Manager** or **Menu Manager** or any other manager screen and clicking on **New**.

Again, a small interface change, but a giant leap for content managers! This improvement will definitely save you many unnecessary clicks in your day-to-day site management routine. By clicking on the *Add New...* fly-out menu item, you get to the "Create Something New" screen in one go.

Several menu items now contain this extra fly-out menu option. If they do, this is indicated by a little blue arrow pointing right, as shown below:

Timesaver # 3: Save & New

In Joomla! 1.5, the backend toolbar allowed you to **Save** (for example an article, or a new menu item), **Apply** (to save your work without closing the screen), or **Close** the screen without saving changes. In Joomla! 1.6, there's a new button called **Save & New**. When you hit this button while editing an article, it saves your changes, closes the article, and opens a blank article screen.

Using the new Save & New button

Let's find out how using **Save & New** can help you to work faster. Imagine you want to get started adding content to your website and make room for new articles. This requires a set of new categories. In this exercise, you will add a series of categories:

1. Navigate to **Content | Category Manager.** A second-level menu item will appear: **Add new category.** Click on this menu item to open the **Add New Category** screen:

2. In the **Title** field, enter **New category #1**.

3. There is no need to change any other details just now, so you're ready to save the category. However, you don't have to click on **Save** . Click on **Save & New** instead.

4. A new, empty **Add New Category** screen appears, confirming that you've successfully saved the category you just made:

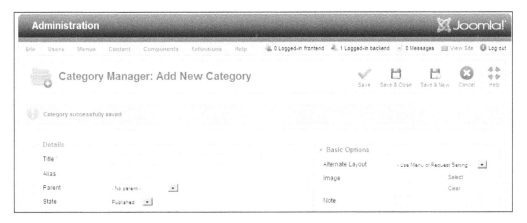

5. Enter the **Title** of the second category and click on **Save & New** again.

6. Repeat *Step 5* for all of the new categories you need. When you've entered the last **Title** of the new category you need to create, click on **Save & Close**. You're taken to the **Category Manager**.

The result is displayed in the **Category Manager**. If you don't see your new categories in the first screen, click on the **Next** button at the bottom of the screen to discover the latest additions:

Timesaver # 4: Save as Copy

You've experienced that the **Save & New** feature enables you to create series of new items with lightning speed. Now what's the difference with the other new toolbar feature, called **Save as Copy**? Hitting this button not only saves the current article, but leaves the current screen and its contents open for you to edit a copy of the article you have just saved.

Creating dummy content using Save as Copy

The **Save as Copy** button will help you when you need to create items that have much in common, such as categories that share a specific combination of settings or articles that all have the same dummy content and are only different in their title and categories. Let's find out how this last example can benefit you in real life, when you need to set up a new website and include a series of dummy articles fast:

1. Go to **Content | Article Manager** and click on the new fly-out submenu item **Add new article**:

2. In the **Add New Article** screen, enter the article **Title** and some **Article Text**. In this example, we'll leave the other settings unchanged, but you could choose any combination of settings needed:

3. As you can see in the previous screenshot, there's still no such thing as a **Save as Copy** button. This is because the current article hasn't been saved yet. To do this now, click on the **Save** button.

4. A message is displayed: **Article successfully saved**. Moreover, a new **Save as Copy** button appears:

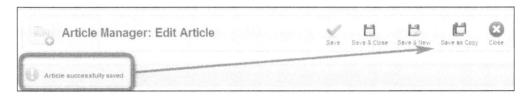

5. Your first article is now saved. Just change whatever you need to change now for the second article. Changing just the **Title** is enough, although you should also delete the contents of the **Alias** area. These contents are filled in by Joomla! automatically, but you have to delete them to force Joomla! to recreate the **Alias** to match your new article title. (If you don't clear the **Alias** field or enter a new alias manually, Joomla! will display an error message telling you that a new article can't have the same alias as an existing one).

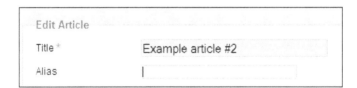

6. Now click on **Save as Copy**. The copy with the new article **Title (Example article #2)** has been saved.

7. Repeat the previous two steps to create as many copies as you like. When you're done creating the last copy, click on **Save & Close**.

8. You're taken to the **Article Manager**. Click on the word **Date** at the top of the **Date** column; this will sort the articles by date and show the most recently added articles on top. Your set of new articles is displayed as shown next:

Timesaver # 5: tabbed screens

When you're working with categories, chances are at some point you'll want to switch to the articles screen to add some content to the categories you've just managed. Previously, this would involve clicking around in the backend interface, closing one screen and opening another. In Joomla! 1.6, this is much easier thanks to the introduction of tabbed screens as shown below. Each tab opens its own screen with new content.

 In the default backend template called Bluestork, Joomla!'s tabs don't actually look like the tabs as used in other software or on websites. Normally, a tab isn't displayed separately from its own screen, whereas Joomla! tabs are. However, they function as tabs: whatever option you click, defines what content is shown below it.

When you're working with categories, there are two tabs that allow you to quickly jump to screens with related functionality: **Articles** and **Featured Articles**.

You'll find tabbed screens in many different places in the backend. When working with **Menus** you can quickly jump to **Menu Items**, and when managing **Users** you can instantly switch to **User Groups** and **Access Levels**.

One great life-saver: two-step deletion

In Joomla! 1.5, it was possible to accidentally remove things in the backend. You could inadvertently delete other items, such as sections or categories, by just one unlucky click of the mouse.

Joomla! 1.6 features a new safety system to prevent backend users deleting articles and menu items by mistake. It's comparable to the trash can system found on most computer operating systems: to delete items, you send them to the trash can, and to delete them permanently, you empty the trash. Previously, this two-step trashing was only implemented for menu items and articles. Now, any item that you want to delete has to be deleted in two steps. This is a great safety feature.

Moreover, the steps involved trashing, deleting, or recovering have changed a little since Joomla! 1.5. Let's find out how this works.

Deleting an item

Let's delete a category from the Joomla! sample data:

1. Navigate to **Content | Category Manager** and select the category called **Joomla!**. Click on the **Trash** button in the toolbar:

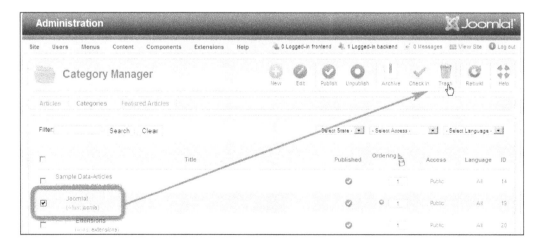

2. A message appears to confirm the deletion. You're done.

Inspect the category list to make sure that the **Joomla!** category has effectively disappeared from the category list.

Exploring and restoring thrashed content

In Joomla! 1.6, there's a new way to find out what items have been sent to the Trash. You can find Trash information in the Manager screens of the backend:

1. To explore trashed categories, go to the the **Category Manager**. In the **Select State** drop-down box, select **Trash**:

2. The **Category Manager** screen now displays only trashed content. In this case, the **Joomla!** category which you've just deleted is shown. In the **Published** column, a trash can icon is displayed, indicating the category's state:

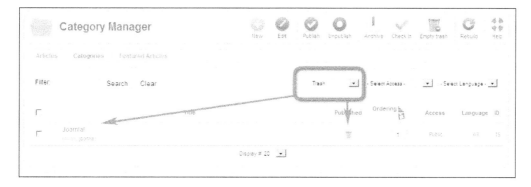

3. To undo the deletion and restore the category, click on the trash can icon in the **Published** column. The **Joomla!** category disappears from the list and a message is displayed: **1 category successfully published**.

   Another way to perform the same action is to select the **Joomla!** category and click on the **Publish** button in the toolbar.

4. To check if the **Joomla!** category has been published again, in the **Select State** drop-down box, select **Published**:

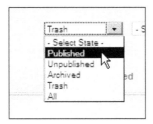

The deleted category is now listed again among the **Category Manager** items.

Permanently deleting items

To permanently delete categories that have been sent to the trash, follow these two steps. Be careful, as there's no undoing a permanent deletion!

1. To explore trashed categories, go to the **Category Manager**. In the **Select State** drop-down box, select **Trash** to display all trashed contents.

2. Select the trashed category — in this example it's **Joomla!** — and click on **Empty Trash** in the toolbar:

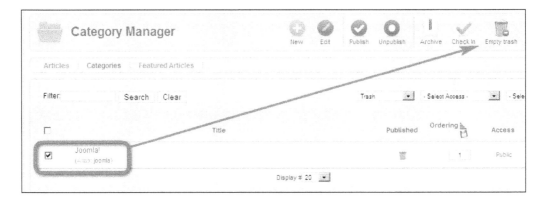

The category has now been deleted permanently.

Changes in Joomla! lingo

Whenever you would set your preferences in Joomla! 1.5, whether creating an article, managing a menu, or administering a module, you had to endure a strange example of Joomla! lingo: parameters. This was a technical term that really just meant 'settings' or 'options'. In 1.6, the infamous parameters have been renamed options.

When browsing the backend, you'll notice there are more minor improvements in the backend naming conventions. The goal of the developers has clearly been to phrase things in a way that's more meaningful to first time users.

Customizing the looks of the backend

Joomla! 1.5 came with just one template to be used in the administrator backend. In 1.6, you can choose between the default template (called Bluestork) and an alternative called Hathor. The latter isn't just any other template: it's fully accessible. This means that it has been built according to accessibility rules, allowing people of all abilities and disabilities to have equal access to the site. For instance, an accessible template enables blind users to navigate the site using screen readers (text-to-speech software).

The layout of the Hathor template stays close to the default template, which means that it's easy to switch without having to learn to use a different layout.

Selecting another backend template

1. To try out Hathor, navigate to **Extensions | Template Manager**. The **Template Manager : Styles** screen is displayed. In the **Location** column, two templates are indicated to be **Administrator** templates: **Bluestork** and **Hathor**. An orange star in the **Default** column indicates that Bluestork is the current template for the site backend:

2. To set Hathor as the default administrator template, click on the grey star to the right of the template name, located in the **Default** column:

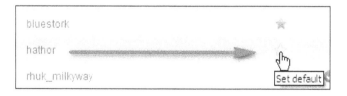

3. The Hathor template becomes active immediately. A message appears: **Default style successfully set**:

Take some time to explore Hathor. All of the backend functionality is the same. If you're familiar with the Joomla! backend interface, you won't have to get used to Hathor: the one main layout change is that the toolbar buttons are now placed on the left-hand side on the screen. Hathor may look a little less refined than the default template, but it's fast and clearly laid out and easy to use.

Setting the backend template to suit your taste

The Hathor template comes with a set of built-in options, enabling you to customize the looks to your taste and needs. Let's find out how to set Hathor to use high contrast colors. This high contrast colors mode is meant to enhance legibility for people with a visual impairment, but other people might find this color scheme easier too:

1. In the **Template Manager : Styles** screen, click on the name of the template.

2. You're taken to the **Template Manager: Edit Style** screen. Here you can set some **Basic Options**. In the **Select Color** drop-down box, select **High Contrast**:

3. Click on **Save & Close** to see the output:

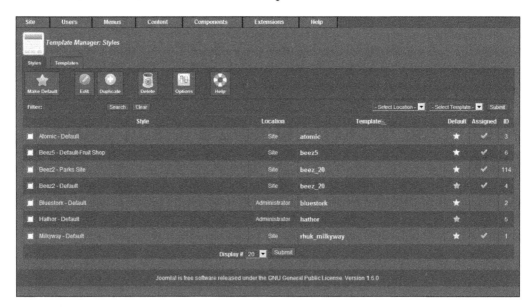

The main color of the backend is now dark blue with white and yellow typography. To switch back to the default template again, navigate to **Extensions | Template Manager** and click on the star next to the Bluestork interface name, in the **Default** column. The template will instantly change back to normal.

Changing Bluestork options

It's also possible to change basic settings in the default backend template, Bluestork. Click on the name **Bluestork** in the **Template Manager** to access the **Template Manager: Edit Style** page. The **Basic Options** presented here allow you, among other things, to determine whether you want to use bigger text (for enhanced legibility), and whether the site name should be displayed in the black top bar of the backend template interface.

Summary

- It's a tiny detail, but it's a great safety improvement: you can now change a custom administrator username when installing Joomla! – that is, before you first enter the backend interface.

- The changes in the Joomla! 1.6 backend interface are more than skin deep. The backend interface has been reorganized. Some menu items have been reorganized to make them more logical and easier to use. New shortcuts to the backend home page or to other frequently used screens are among the great little timesavers.

- The **Save & New** and **Save as Copy** buttons help you create new content very efficiently, allowing you to skip a few clicks in the process.

- Joomla! 1.6 features a new safety system to prevent you accidentally deleting articles and menu items: deleting in two steps, using the **Trash** and **Empty Trash** buttons.

- Finally, new backend templates and template options allow you to customize the looks of the backend – to enhance the legibility and usability, or just to make it look more beautiful.

In the next chapter, we'll get to the heart of the matter: managing content. You'll learn all about one of the most significant improvements in Joomla! 1.6, organizing content using nested categories.

3
Organizing and Managing Content

Joomla! 1.6 makes creating, managing, and organizing content easier in many respects. One of the main improvements is that Joomla! now allows you to categorize articles any way you like. The rigid old section and category system has been replaced by a more powerful content categorization system, called "nested categories". But there are many more improvements in the backend, making it easier to create and organize articles.

In this chapter, you'll learn about the benefits of Joomla!'s new content management features. We'll cover the following topics:

- Organizing content using nested categories
- Adding category notes and category metadata
- New ways to display category contents on the site
- Creating and editing content: using the updated article editor
- Archiving and un-archiving articles

Organizing content using nested categories

Anyone who's used to working with the previous versions of Joomla! knows the old section — category — article drill. Articles had to be part of a category and categories had to be part of a section. There were no workarounds for this rigid three-level content organization scheme. Sometimes, this required Joomla! users to adapt their content to the system's limitations (or extend Joomla!'s functionality by using more powerful content management extensions, so-called Content Construction Kits or CCKs).

In Joomla! 1.6, the rigid old system has finally been replaced. Sections have gone; there are now only categories, and any category can hold as many levels of subcategories as you need. In the backend, instead of both a **Section Manager** and a **Category Manager**, you'll now find only a **Category Manager**. You can forget the concept of sections altogether; in Joomla!! 1.6 there's no need for them anymore, as they're no longer needed as 'containers' to hold categories.

Improvement #1: categories can now be one level deep

Sometimes, you'll want to organize articles in just one category. Let's say you want to add a few articles about your organization: who you are, where to reach you, and so on. You don't need any subcategories. You'd need a structure like this:

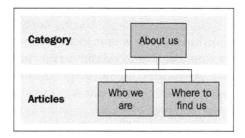

In Joomla! 1.5, this simple setup of a "sectionless" category holding articles wasn't possible. You'd have to organize content in sections and categories—which implied that any group of articles would be stored two levels deep, even if you didn't need this. The only alternative was *not to organize content, using uncategorized articles.*

In Joomla! 1.6, you can put content in just one category if you want to. Just go to **Content | Category Manager | Add New Category** to create a new category. In the **Parent** drop down box, select **No parent**:

As this category has "**No parent**", it becomes a top-level or "parent" category. It's as simple as that; now you can do something that wasn't possible in Joomla! 1.5, by assigning articles directly to this category.

Improvement #2: creating multiple category levels

Joomla!'s old section—category—article approach didn't allow you to create categories within categories ("nested categories"). However, on content-rich sites, you might need more than two levels of content organization and use a few subcategories. Here's an example from a site featuring product reviews. It uses several levels to organize the main category of "reviews" in subcategories of product types, brands, and models:

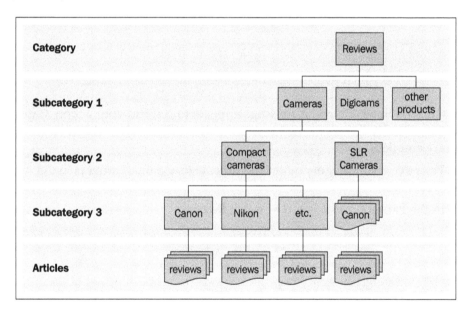

A great advantage of being able to create such a structure is that it allows for very specific searches (that is, within categories) and multiple ways of navigation. Another example is if you are creating a catalog that you want to be searchable with multiple filters such as manufacturer, price, general item type, or a specific product name.

Creating a set of 'nested' categories

Let's find out how you can quickly set up a few nested categories like the ones shown in the illustration above:

1. Go to **Content | Category Manager | Add New Category**.

2. In the **Title** field, enter **Reviews**.

3. In the **Parent** field, make sure that the default option **No parent** is selected. The screen should look like this:

4. Click on **Save & New**. A message appears to confirm your action: **Category successfully saved**. At the same time, all the fields in the **Add New Category** are emptied.

5. To create a subcategory, enter the subcategory name **Cameras** in the **Title** field.

6. In the **Parent** drop-down box, select **Reviews**:

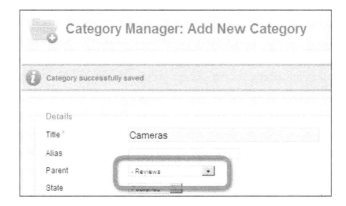

7. Click on **Save & New** to store the subcategory.

8. Repeat the previous three steps to create more subcategories. For each new category, first enter a title, then select the appropriate parent category and save it by clicking on **Save & New**.

9. When you're done with creating subcategories, click on **Save & Close** to view the results in the Category Manager. In the example below, the **Cameras** category is parent to a subcategory **Compact Cameras**. The **Compact Cameras** category is parent to a subcategory called **Canon**.

If you've followed the above example, you'll find the following set of categories in the **Category Manager**. They are displayed as shown below:

The **Reviews** name isn't indented, as it is a top-level category. **Cameras**, **Compact Cameras**, and **Canon** are displayed indented as they are subcategories.

When you create articles, you can now assign them to the new categories. The same category hierarchy as you've just seen in the **Category Manager** is displayed in the **Category** drop-down box:

Using nested categories in the sample data

You've just set up a few categories and subcategories yourself. On a complex site, you can have a far more complex structure. Don't worry, I won't ask you to create dozens of nested categories right now — but it's a good idea to learn from the example set by the Joomla! Developers. Let's have a look at the categories and articles that come with Joomla! when it is installed with sample data. The way things are organized there will give you some idea of how you can deploy nested categories and get the most out of the new system.

Exploring the sample data

1. On the frontend, click on the **Sample sites** link in the **This Site** menu.

2. On the **Sample Sites** page, a new menu appears. This menu gives access to both sample sites — **Australian Parks** and **Fruit Shop**:

Have a look around at both example sites. They appear to be separate websites, but they're not. Here the Joomla! developers have cunningly deployed the possibilities of the new category system and have organized all content for the three sites (the main site and two example sites) within one big website. To find out how this is done, let's have a look at the categories in the backend:

1. Go to **Content | Category Manager** to see how the sample content is organized. The screenshot below shows an overview:

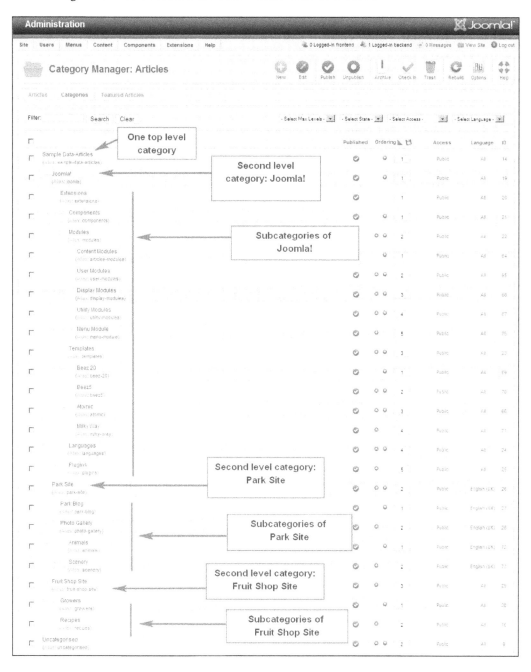

As you can see in the screenshot above, there's one top-level category, **Sample Data-Articles**. All other articles are contained in the subcategories of this main level category. Apart from the top level category, there are three main categories:

- The **Joomla!** category. It has three sublevels.
- The **Park Site** category. It has two sublevels.
- The **Fruit Shop** category. It has one sublevel.

Finally, there's a group of articles that's not in any category; it's a bunch of leftovers all marked as Uncategorized.

How can different categories look like different sites?

As you click through the example sites, not only the content changes; the menu links to each main category (such as the Parks and Fruit Shop category) have specific templates assigned to them. This way, on the frontend, the look-and-feel of the different main article categories are totally different, whereas in the backend, they're just part of one big site.

Applying templates to categories can give visitors the impression of exploring a separate set of websites. You'll learn more about assigning templates to specific site parts in *Chapter 6*.

Although there's no limit to the number of levels in the category hierarchy, even in this rather complex set of sample site articles, categories don't go further than four levels deep. It is possible to make more subcategories, but keep in mind that this means that your content will be stored 'deeper' in the hierarchy, possibly making it more difficult for visitors (and search engines) to find it.

One benefit of placing interrelated content under its own main level category is that you can easily unpublish, delete, or archive any content dealing with a specific subject by unpublishing, deleting, or archiving this main level category. That's why the Joomla! developers have chosen to use one top-level category for all sample data. By unpublishing the top level category (Sample Data-Articles), you can unpublish all of the example content in one go.

New category settings: notes and metadata

When entering or editing a new category, the **New** Category or **Edit** Category screen now offer you an area to type notes about the purpose of the category or related items, as well as a place to add keywords and a description (metadata).

The **Note** field (found in the **Basic Options** section) can be useful to share some extra information about the category with other backend users. For example, you can enter a short explanation about this category ('subcategory of ...'):

Adding category metadata

In Joomla! 1.5, there was no way to separately enter metadata for category pages. Now, you can enter specific **Meta Description** and **Meta Keywords** in the **Metadata Options** section when creating or editing a category. To find out more on using these metadata fields, see *Chapter 8* on SEO improvements in Joomla! 1.6:

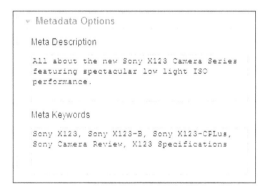

Another new item in the **Basic Options** of a category is the **Alternative Layout** select box. Alternative layouts are an advanced new feature that enable you to select a customized layout for the current category, provided the selected template (or a third-party component) provides these extra layout options. A template can contain so-called template override files, allowing for customized layouts that replace Joomla!'s default views. Using the **Alternative Layout** select box, you can now select the template override you want to activate for this particular item. To find out more about this feature, have a look at the "Introduction to Alternative Layouts in Version 1.6" document on the Joomlacode site. You'll find it at `http://downloads.joomlacode.org/ trackeritem/5/8/6/58619/introtoaltlayoutsinversion1- 6v2.pdf`.

Fresh ways to display category contents on the frontend

Joomla! 1.6 provides several additional methods to display category contents. They replace the four classic layouts of **Category List**, **Category Blog**, **Section List**, and **Section Blog**. When creating a new menu link pointing to a category, you are now presented with a slightly different set of Menu Item Types:

These are the category views are available:

- **List All Categories** is a new view, described below
- **Category Blog** was previously called Category Blog Layout
- **Category List** was previously called Category List Layout

The Blog and List views are basically the same as they've always been. However, these display types now offer new settings that provide more control over the look and feel of the resulting pages.

Along with the new **List All Categories** menu item type, there are also a few new module types that provide you with new ways to display links to categories and their article contents. Let's have a closer look at the new category views.

New category view # 1: List All Categories

The new category system rationalizes the organization of content, even in large or complex websites. One advantage of this is that you can more easily give visitors (and search engines!) access to all that well-structured content, just by adding one menu link to a main level category. This will allow visitors to easily drill down the different layers (the category levels) of the site structure.

To achieve this, the new **List All Categories** menu link type allows you to display categories as well as their subcategory contents. You can see an example of this menu organization if you select the **Site Map** link on the **This Site** menu in the frontend of the sample Joomla! 1.6 content. As we've previously seen, the sample data that comes with Joomla! 1.6 is organized in a structured way. The **Site Map** link uses the **List All Categories** menu item type to show all levels in the category hierarchy.

Creating a link to a site map

Let's find out how you can set up a site map link yourself. We'll create a basic site map to present links to all articles on the site:

1. Go to **Menus | Main Menu**.

2. Click on **New**. In the **Menu Manager: New Menu Item** screen, click on the **Select** button to open the **Select a Menu Item Type** popup window. Select **List All Categories**:

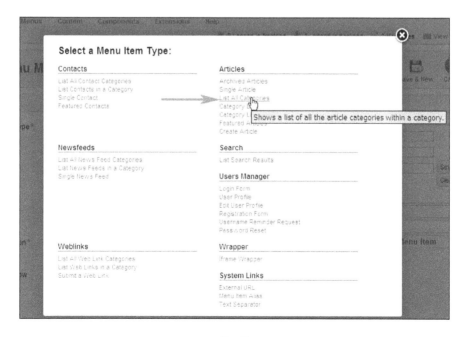

The pop up window closes.

3. In the **Menu Title** field, enter **Articles Site Map**.

4. In the **Required Settings** section, the default value in the **Select a Top Level Category** drop-down list is **Root**. You'll probably want to leave this unchanged, as a typical site map should display the contents of all the categories from the site top level.

5. In the **Categories Options** panel, we'll make a few changes to the default settings to ensure that the site map will only display a tree of category names. In the **Subcategories Descriptions** drop-down box, select **Hide**. In the **# Articles in Category** drop-down box, select **Hide** too. This way, Joomla! won't display the category descriptions (entered when creating or editing a category) and the number of articles in the categories.

6. Click on **Save** and click on **View Site** to see the output on the frontend. A new link is added to the main menu: **Articles Site Map**. Click on this link to see the site map:

This is all there is to creating a site map for all article content on the site. Creating a menu link of the **List All Categories** Menu Item Type using all the default options will result in a page displaying a list of links to the categories and their contents.

Tweaking the site map display

When creating a **List All Categories** link, on the right-hand side of the screen you'll see a bunch of options panels. It's worth trying out the available settings, as they result in pages that look quite different (although they all basically serve the same purpose, creating links to different levels of category contents). As an example, have a go at changing the **Categories Options**. These allow you to fine-tune the site map layout and display.

To make the site map a little easier for human visitors to use, in the **Categories Options** you might want to add some descriptive text to the various categories. If you'd like to try this out, you can edit the site map menu link that you've created in the previous exercise and enter the following details in the **Categories Options**:

- Set **Top Level Category Description** to **Show**.

- In the **Top Level Category Description** box, add a short explanatory text that will be displayed at the top of the Site Map page, such as "**Looking for a particular article? Browse this site map, listing all the articles.**"

- To make sure all subcategories are displayed, set **Subcategory Levels** to **All**.

- To display descriptive texts introducing individual categories, set **Subcategories Descriptions** to **Show**. This way, descriptions that have been entered for individual categories (through **Content | Category Manager | New/Edit**) will be displayed on the site map page.

When you've changed the settings as described above, the options panel should look like this:

- To check the effect of these changes, click on **Save** and then click on **View Site**.

  The **Articles Site Map** link in the Main Menu now still displays links to all categories, but you'll notice that more details (such as descriptions of category contents) have been added:

Adding descriptions can be helpful to your visitors, as they can explain the various categories on your site, instead of just presenting the category names as a list of hyperlinks.

 As site maps come, the **List All Categories** menu item type produces a very basic one. There are third-party extensions specifically aimed at creating site maps. These will include more content (not just articles) and have more features. Consult the Joomla! extensions directory to see what's available: `http://extensions.joomla.org/extensions/structure-a-navigation/site-map`.

New Category View # 2: Articles Categories Module

Joomla! 1.6 features two other new methods to present category contents. Two new modules are available, allowing you to show (links to) categories and their contents in module positions or embedded in articles. The new modules are:

- Articles Categories Module, which displays a list of the names of categories (from one parent category) as hyperlinks

- Articles Category module, which shows what articles are contained in one or more categories

The names of these modules may confuse you. Actually, it's better to think of the second module as the Articles in Category module, because that's exactly what it does; it shows what articles are contained in one or more categories. First, we'll look into the possibilities of the Articles Categories module; after that, we'll explore the Articles Category module.

Creating an Articles Categories module

The Articles Categories module is a simple little navigational aid, allowing you to display links to children of the current category. Let's use this module to display a list of categories we want to draw the visitor's attention to:

1. Go to **Extensions | Module Manager**. Click on **New**.

2. In the pop up window, select **Articles Categories**:

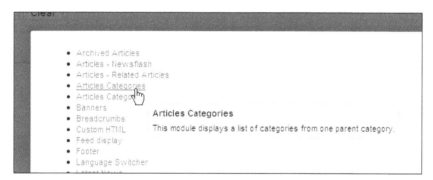

3. In the **Title** field, enter **All about extensions**.

4. Set **Show Title** to **Show**.

5. In the **Position** drop-down box, select **position-9**.

6. In the **Basic Options** panel, select **Extensions** as the **Parent Category**. The other options allow you to customize the module display, but we'll leave the default settings unchanged.

7. In the **Menu Assignment** section, change a few settings to make the module display only on the home page:
   - Select **Module Assignment: Only on the pages selected**
   - Now click on **Toggle selection** to deselect all the pages
   - Click on the **Main Menu** tab and select the **Home** link
   - The module screen should look as shown below:

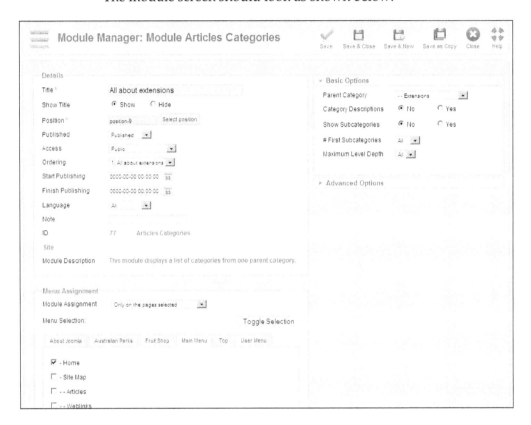

8. Click on **Save & Close** and then click on **View Site** to see the output:

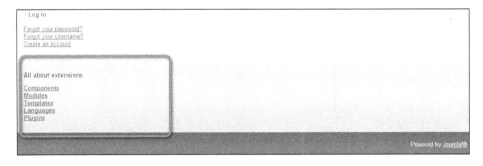

The left-most of the three bottom panels on the frontend of the site now contains a listing of categories in the extensions main category.

> You'll notice that the three panels have only turned up now that we've assigned a module to them. That's because the default Joomla! 1.6 template, Beez 2, contains code to check if there's any content assigned to the position-9, position-10, and position-11 positions. These positions represent the row of panels below the main content. This row of panels is only displayed if any of these panels contain content.

Adding some more category listings

To add two more category listings to the three panels at the bottom of the screen, follow these steps. We'll add more instances of the same module, this time displaying categories within the Templates category and the Park Site category:

1. Create a new **Articles Categories** module as described above. In the **Title** field, enter **All about templates**.

2. In the **Parent Category** drop-down box, select **Templates**.

3. In the **Position** drop-down box, select **position-10**. This is the middle panel position.

4. Again, set the module to display only on the homepage and save it.

5. Finally, create a third new **Articles Categories** module. In the **Title** field, enter **Park Site Categories**.

6. In the **Parent Category** drop-down box, select **Park Site**.

7. In the **Position** drop down box, select **position-11**. This is the right panel position.

8. Again, set the module to display only on the homepage and save it.

The output should look as displayed in the following screenshot:

New Category View # 3: Articles (in) Category Module

Apart from the Articles Categories module (displaying category names), there's another new module to display category contents: **Articles Category**. What's the difference? This new module may seem a modest new feature, but it's amazingly powerful—and very much more so than the module that resembles it only in name, Articles Categories. It makes it possible to present category contents in a variety of ways.

Using the new Articles Category Module

As an example, let's create a list of teaser texts pointing the visitor to articles in the Modules category:

1. Go to **Extensions | Module Manager** and click on **New**.

2. In the pop up window, select **Articles Category**:

- Archived Articles
- Articles - Newsflash
- Articles - Related Articles
- Articles Categories
- Articles Category
- Banners
- Breadcrumbs   **Articles Category**
- Custom HTML
- Feed display   This module displays a list of articles from one or more categories.
- Footer

3. In the **Title** field, enter **More on modules**.

4. In the **Position** drop-down list, select **position-8**. This way the module will be displayed in a column on the right-hand side.

5. In the **Menu Assignment** section, change a few settings to make the module display only on the home page:

    ° Select **Module Assignment: Only on the pages selected**.

    ° Now click on **Toggle selection** to deselect all the pages.

    ° Click on the **Main Menu** tab and select the **Home** link.

6. Now let's set the **Options** to get the module to display what we want, how we want it:

    ° Click on the **Filtering options** heading to display the available options in this panel.

    ° In the **Category** list, select the **Modules** category as shown in the screenshot below.

    ° Leave **Category Filtering Type** set to **Inclusive** as shown in the screenshot below. This way, only contents from the selected category will be displayed. (If set to **Exclusive**, all categories but the selected ones would be displayed).

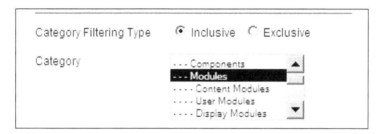

7. Set **Child Category Articles** to **Include**. If we'd leave this set to **Exclude**, only articles in the selected category (Modules) would be displayed – but this category doesn't itself contain any articles! Its child categories do. By selecting **Include**, we make sure that the articles contained in the subcategories get displayed.

8. Click on **Save** and then click on **View site** to see the output on the frontend:

- We've obviously created a rather huge list of links to articles that are all part of the Modules subcategories. Let's change this to set a maximum number of five links. We'll customize the display further to add the article intro texts, instead of just the article titles.

9. Return to the **Articles Category** module edit screen. In the **Grouping** options, set **Article Grouping** to **Category**. In the **Display Options**, set **Introtext** to **Show** and keep **Introtext limit** set to **100** to display the first 100 characters of the article text.

10. In the **Filtering** options, you can limit the number of items to be displayed. Set **Count** to **6** to display a maximum of six articles.

11. Click on **Save** and then click on **View site** to see the results:

The category contents are now displayed ordered by category. All the articles contain a short teaser text.

Take some time to explore the many options of the Articles Category module. In the **Filtering Options**, you can filter by author (that is, display only contents written by specific authors), you can exclude certain articles by entering their article ID's, you can filter by date (to show articles that have been published within a date range field, or articles written in (for example) the last 30 days. In the **Display Options**, you can choose to show article details (such as the category name or creation date).

Working with the updated article editor

Creating or editing an article in Joomla! 1.6 will seem very familiar to 1.5 users. Go to **Content | Article Manager | New** or **Edit** to display the article editor screen:

On closer inspection, you'll notice some items have been renamed or rearranged:

- In the **New Article** section, you can set the article to be **Featured**. This is just another word for what was previously called 'Front Page' or 'Show on Front Page'.

- In the **Article Options**, references to sections have gone. The **Show Category** option allows you to show the Category Title of the current category. The **Show Parent** option allows you to also show the parent category title among the article details.

- In the **Article Options**, references to sections have gone. The **Show Category** option allows you to show the Category Title of the current category. The **Show Parent** option allows you to also show the parent category title among the article details.

- In the **New Article** section, there's a **Permissions** button that jumps to the separate **Article Permissions** section at the bottom of the screen. As you can see, the new user permissions options are available on many levels in the Joomla! 1.6 interface. Here you can set user permissions to delete or edit the current article. You'll learn more about user permissions in *Chapter 5*.

Creating a link to an article

It may seem a simple task, but in previous versions it was a bit of a hassle to create a link to from one article to another in the same website. You had to install a different editor (such as JCE) or a dedicated extension (such as Linkr) to get the job done easily. In Joomla! 1.6, this has been fixed. Below the article editor screen, you'll find a new button called **Article**:

When you use this button to insert an article link, Joomla! will automatically include the link text. In other words, it inserts the title of the destination page as the new hyperlink text.

Inserting an article title as a hyperlink

Let's create a hyperlink to another article in the sample site:

1. Go to **Content | Article Manager** and open the article in which you want to add a hyperlink. As an example, you can select the **Administrator Components** article.

2. In the article editor screen, place the mouse cursor anywhere in the article where you want the new link text to appear.

3. Click on the **Article** button to open a pop up screen containing a list with all the articles in the site. If you don't see the destination article, scroll through the list to find it. In the example below, we select the article titled **Australian Parks**:

4. Click on the title of the article. The pop up window closes and the article title is inserted into the current article as a hyperlink:

5. Save the article to commit the changes.

Tweaking the link text

Using the **Article** button, the text link that you enter automatically consists of the title of the target page. Now what if you want the actual link text to be different from the article title? Just select the link text (in the example we've just covered, select the **Austrialian Parks** text) and edit the highlighted text. Any text you enter will still remain a hyperlink:

Using the updated Media Manager

In 1.6, the Media Manager has been moved from its former location on the **Site** menu to the **Content** menu — which is logical, as uploading and managing is something very closely related to managing article content.

Let's find out how you can enhance the functionality of the Media Manager by changing just one setting and enabling the multiple upload feature. This enables you to upload multiple image files in one go, instead of having to upload one file, selecting another one, and so on. In Joomla! 1.5, this Flash-powered feature didn't function reliably — now it's fixed.

Enabling the Flash image uploader

1. To change **Media Manager** settings, click on the **Options** button in the Media Manager toolbar:

Media Manager

2. Clicking on the **Options** button brings up the **Media Manager Options** pop up screen. Here you can enhance the Media Manager functionality by enabling the feature to upload multiple image files in one go. By default, this is turned off. Change the default setting in the **Enable Flash uploader** field to **Yes**:

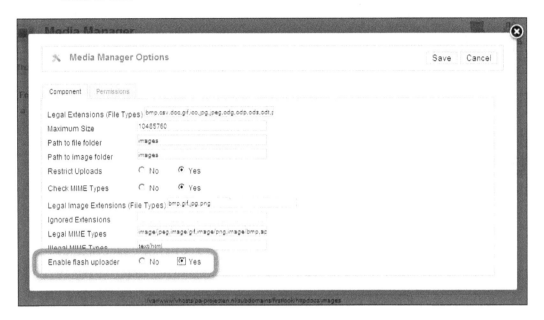

3. The **Upload files** section in the **Media Manager** screen will change to show a few enhanced options:

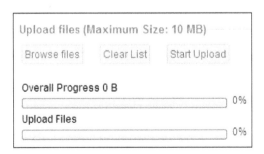

4. To see how this works, click on **Browse files** to select multiple files from your computer's hard drive. The selected files will appear in a file list below the **Upload Files** progress bar:

5. In the **Files** screen, select the target folder where you want to store the new image files. (You can also make a new folder by clicking on **Create Folder.**)

6. Once you've selected the files to be uploaded and the target folder, start uploading the files by clicking on **Start Upload**. The Flash Uploader displays the upload progress:

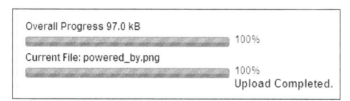

Once uploaded, your image files are ready to be inserted through the article editor **Insert Image** button.

Archiving articles

As your site grows, you may want to clean up the site contents. You probably don't want to display outdated articles — such as last year's news — among your current content. In Joomla!, there are a few ways to achieve this. You can unpublish old articles. That way, the articles are still available in the backend, but the site visitor cannot see them anymore. Another option is to create an archive. Archived articles are still available, but they're no longer part of the "normal" site contents. You can make them visible through a menu link of the **Archived Articles** menu item type.

Archiving is something you do by hand; there's no way to automatically archive articles that are older than a given period of time. To archive an article (or multiple articles at once), select the desired articles in the **Article Manager** and click on the **Archive** toolbar button.

This process hasn't changed since Joomla! 1.5. However, you can now also change the article **State** to **Archived** when you've opened it in the article editor screen:

To see which articles have been archived, go to the Article Manager and select **Archived** in the **State** select box:

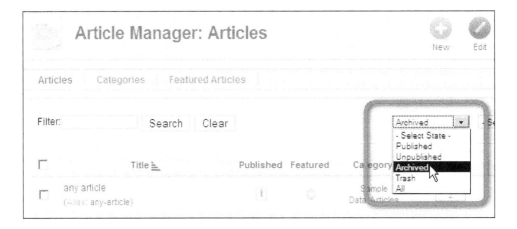

In 1.5, you couldn't edit Archived Articles; you needed to first change their state to Published or Unpublished, edit the article, and then re-archive it. In 1.6, you can directly edit an archived article. This is quite useful. After all, although articles are archived, you might still want to correct a typo or delete some outdated information. To edit an archived article, just click on the article **Title** in the Article Manager to open the **Article Manager: Edit Article** screen.

To de-archive an article, select the article and change the **State** from Archived to **Published** (or **Unpublished**, if you don't want to display the article). Click on **Save** to commit the state change.

Summary

In this chapter, we've focused on what it's all about in Joomla!: managing actual content. You've seen how Joomla! 1.6 enables you to categorize content and to display category contents, and you've learned what's new in creating and editing content:

- The biggest change in working with content is the new way in which articles can be organized in an unlimited number of categories and subcategories.

- The **New** Category or **Edit** Category screen offers you some new settings, such as adding a note or adding metadata for category pages.

- There are some flexible new methods available to display category contents on the frontend of your site: through the **Display All Categories** menu item type, and through two new modules displaying links to categories and articles.

- The updated article editor screen now allows you to easily create a link from one article to another in the same website.

- The Media Manager, Joomla!'s built-in utility to upload and manage image files, is now located at **Content | Media Manager**. You can enhance the functionality of the Media Manager by enabling the multiple upload feature, the so-called Flash Uploader.

- A useful improvement in the way Joomla! handles archived articles, is that you can now directly edit an archived article.

In this chapter, you've had an overview of the changes in the way you organize, manage, and create content in Joomla! 1.6. In *Chapter 4*, we'll look into another major aspect of content management: making it all accessible through menu navigation. We'll find out what's new in managing menus and menu items.

4
Managing Menus and Menu Modules

When Joomla! 1.6 was announced, most attention went to major changes and additions, such as the new content categorization system that we covered in the previous chapter. However, there are many more little changes that result in almost equally important improvements in your user experience as a Joomla! site administrator. Good examples of this are the changes in the Joomla! Menu Manager. You'll be surprised to experience how a set of relatively small changes enhances the way you manage menus and menu items.

These are the topics that we'll cover in this chapter:

- Using the new **Menu Manager** screen
- Managing the contents of menus in the **Menu Items** screen
- Using new Menu Item Types

Goodbye to a spartan Menu Manager

The Menu Manager in Joomla! 1.5 did the job, but there was certainly some room for improvement. Joomla! 1.6 offers a fully overhauled Menu Manager. Just to see why this is a good thing and what's been added, let's have a very brief look at what the old menu manager looked like. Here's the old **Menu Manager** screen:

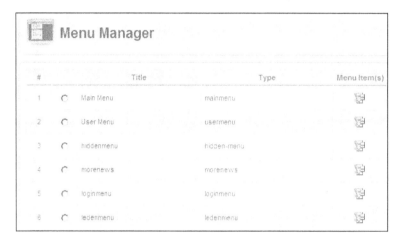

It was a really basic setup—but it didn't function as anyone new to Joomla! would expect. If you'd click any of the menu names in the **Menu Manager** in order to edit the menu links, you'd end up in the wrong screen:

No Joomla!, we didn't want to change the **Unique Name** or any other internal references to the menu! There must be many, many Joomla! users who had to learn the hard way that in order to edit the menu contents, they actually had to click an inconspicuous little icon in the **Menu Item(s)** column. In the new release, those days of Menu Manager usability disasters are finally over!

The all-new tabbed Menu Manager screen

In Joomla! 1.6, the Menu Manager has been improved in many ways. Just as in many other parts of the Joomla! backend, there are new buttons and shortcuts, helping you to perform routine tasks both easier and faster. Let's have a look right now.

Exploring the new Menu Manager

1. Go to **Menus | Menu Manager** to open the **Menu Manager**. Choose the **Menus** tab to open its screen, as shown below:

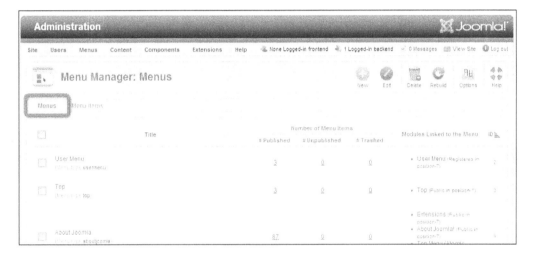

2. You'll notice that the **Menu Manager** screen has been completely redesigned. Near the top of the screen is the tab bar that is common to the new backend interface. The **Menu Manager** screen contains a **Menus** tab and a **Menu Items** tab. The default page, **Menus**, shows an overview of all menus on the site.

3. Just below the **Title** of each menu, you'll notice a slightly smaller hyperlink between brackets, that is **Menu type usermenu**:

4. Click on this link to access secondary **Menu Details**: Joomla!'s internal references to the menu, such as the **Menu Type** and **Description**. This was the screen you'd end up at in Joomla! 1.5 when clicking on the menu name:

5. You probably don't want to change anything here, so click on the **Close** button to return to the **Menu Manager: Menus** screen. Click on the menu **Title** to edit the contents of any menu. Click on the **About Joomla!** menu title to switch to the **Menu Items** screen for this particular menu and show a hierarchical view of its menu contents:

There's another way to jump to the **Menu Items** screen, but it requires an extra click. In the **Menu Manager: Menus** screen, click on the checkbox next to the menu name and choose the **Menu Items** tab to view the menu contents.

So much for our short guided tour through the menu screens. Now let's find out how the changes here will impact you when managing and editing actual menus!

New ways to manage and edit menus

Both the **Menus** screen and the **Menu Items** screen have a better layout structure to make the existing features clearer and easier to access. We'll first take a closer look at two improvements in the **Menus** screen.

A new shortcut to jump straight to selected menu items

The new **Number of Menu Items** column can be very useful, especially when you're working on a large site with many menu items:

Number of Menu Items		
# Published	# Unpublished	# Trashed
3	0	0
3	0	0
90	0	0

The three columns here contain the numbers of menu items that are either **Published**, **Unpublished**, or **Trashed**. Rather than just presenting this as static information, all the numbers function as hyperlinks that instantly take you to the selected set in the **Menu Items** screen. This way, you can easily edit menu items that have been published, unpublished, or thrashed.

These three numbers serve as handy shortcuts to Menu Items that you can also get to by clicking on the **Menu Items** tab and filtering the output there for published, unpublished, or trashed items.

A new shortcut to jump to menu module settings

One of the hardest things to grasp for people starting out using Joomla! is the fact that you have to go to two backend locations to manage menus:

- In the **Menu Manager**, you create and edit menus and the menu contents (the menu links).
- In the **Module Manager**, you control the way the menu is displayed on the site by changing the menu module settings. These are the settings that tell Joomla! how this module is displayed: on what pages, in what position, with or without its title shown, accessible to what user groups, and so on.

In Joomla! 1.6, this principle still holds—but the Menu Manager now provides a new shortcut to Menu Module settings that immediately takes you to the appropriate menu module settings (without you having to first go to another location in the backend and scrolling through a lot of similarly named modules to get to your menu module). In other words, you now control both menu contents and menu module settings without leaving the Menu Manager.

In the **Menu Manager: Menus** screen, this column is the one that will really save a good deal of time:

Let's examine the **Modules Linked to the Menu** column a little more closely. As you can see in the above screenshot, it contains shortcuts to menu modules assigned to the menu, such as **User Menu**, **Top**, and **Extensions**. Moreover, the **Modules Linked to the Menu** column provides a useful overview of relevant module details: without having to click through to explore the module details screen, you're presented with the module title, its access level and its module position (for example **User Menu (Registered in position-7).**

In other words, Joomla! 1.6 provides you with much more information in the **Menu Manager** screen, saving you the trouble of navigating to the Module Manager to find out which menu modules are linked to this particular menu, what the module access level is, or what position on the web page the module has been assigned to.

Changing the menu module settings in the Menu Manager

To find out more about the linked menu modules or to change their settings, just click on the appropriate **Modules Linked to the Menu** shortcut. To find out how this works, we'll change menu settings for the **User Menu** contained in the Joomla! 1.6 sample data:

1. Go to **Menus | Menu Manager**. Locate the **Main Menu**. In the **Modules Linked to the Menu** column, you'll notice that there are four instances of this menu module on this site. It's not only used as the **This Site** menu, but it's also used on other specific pages and positions:

2. To customize the **This Site** menu, click on the hyperlink **This Site (Public in position-7)** in the **Modules Linked to the Menu** column.

3. You're presented with a pop up window in which you can edit module settings. As this is the main menu, let's change the module settings to make the site menu display on a more logical place above the **About Joomla!** menu and to hide the **This Site** menu title (as it's obvious that this is a menu about the site). To do this, set the **Show Title** select box to **Hide**. To make the module appear at the top of the left-hand column, in the **Ordering** drop-down list, select **1. Main Menu**. Click on **Save & Close**.

> You'll notice that the contents of this pop up window are very similar to those you would see if you'd go to **Extensions | Module Manager**, locate the **User Menu** module there, and edit it. In other words, this pop up screen allows you to change settings or enter values without the hassle of leaving the Menu Manager and separately changing the appropriate menu module in the Module Manager.

4. Click on **View Site** to see the output in the frontend. The main menu is now displayed on all pages as the first menu in the left-hand column, right below the header:

What's the Options button about?

In the **Menu Manager: Menus** screen, there's a new button called **Options**:

Clicking on it will open a pop up screen allowing you set all default User Permissions for all menus. Permissions are covered in *Chapter 5*.

New ways to manage and edit menu items

In the previous section, you've seen that Joomla! 1.6 makes it easier to change the settings of menus. But there are also many improvements in the way you work with the menu contents, the actual menu items, found in the **Menu Manager: Menu Items** screen:

Let's have a look at what's new here.

Filtering the list of menu items

When you've got lots of menu items, it's great to be able to filter the menu items list in order to see only the links that are currently relevant. To change the overview of menu items to another selection, the **Menu Items** screen now provides you with five different ways to filter the current list. We'll have a quick look at all of them:

Menu selection filter (About Joomla!)

This nameless filter contains all menu names in alphabetical order. In the example site, the default view of this page will show the **About Joomla!** menu. Instead of having to go back to the **Menus** screen to select another menu, you can use this drop-down list to change the view to the contents of any other menu on the site.

Select Max Levels filter

The **Select Max Levels** filter is really useful when the menu contains many links. For example, the **About Joomla!** menu in the sample site contains about 90 menu links on several levels: the top level, the submenu level, and even third and fourth level links. To get a quick overview of the two top menu levels set the **Max Levels** value to **2**:

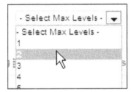

Select State, Access, or Language filter

The **Select State** filter allows you to show items that are either Published, Unpublished, or in the Trash:

Finally, the **Access** and **Language** filters allow you to select items according to their access level or language setting.

Changes in the way you assign a menu item to the homepage

In any site, only one menu item can be set as the one pointing to the default page (home page) of the site. Just as in Joomla! 1.5, you can select any menu item and click on the **Home** button (previously called **Default**) to set this as the home page:

Beginning with Joomla! 1.6, you can change the status of any menu item to **Home** by just clicking on the grey star in the **Home** column. It's easy to make a mistake here: in just one click you can immediately replace the current home page of the site with the page you've selected. If this is not what you want, you can undo this by going to the **Main Menu** and assigning **Home** status to the **Home** menu link again.

New buttons to copy and move menu items

In Joomla! 1.5, you could move or copy menu items from one menu to another by selecting them and clicking on the **Move** or **Copy** button in the Menu Manager toolbar:

These buttons have disappeared in 1.6, but you can still move one or more menu items to another menu. At the bottom of the **Menu Manager: Menu Items** screen, you'll notice a new section called **Batch process the selected menu items**:

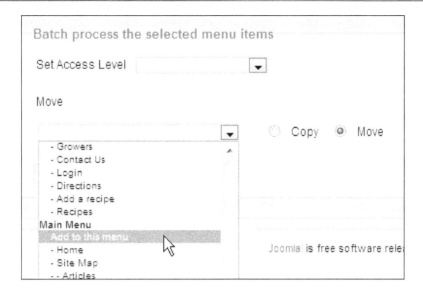

Here you can copy or move all selected menu items to another menu location. Select **Add to this menu** to simply add the new menu links to the menu top level. Select any of the existing menu items to add the new menu links as children (submenu items) of the selected menu item.

> You can also use this **Batch process** section to set the Access Level of selected menu items. Select the desired value in the **Set Access Level** drop-down list and click on the **Process** button. Access Levels and permissions are covered in *Chapter 5*.

Trashing menu items

In *Chapter 2*, you saw that deleting items in Joomla! has changed a little. Previously, to delete menu items, you'd first send them to the trash; after this, you could delete them altogether using the Menu Trash screen. You won't find this screen in Joomla! 1.6 anymore, as Trash is now a state. Items are either Published, Unpublished, or part of the trash. This means that you can delete menu items directly in the **Menu Manager: Menu Items** screen.

Let's find out how you trash and delete menu items the Joomla! 1.6 way:

1. In the **Menu Manager | Menu Items** screen, select the items to be trashed and click on the **Trash** button.

2. To see the menu trash contents, select **Trash** in the **Select State** filter list.

3. Now all thrashed menu items are shown and a new button appears: **Empty Trash**, as shown in the screenshot below. Click on this button to delete selected items:

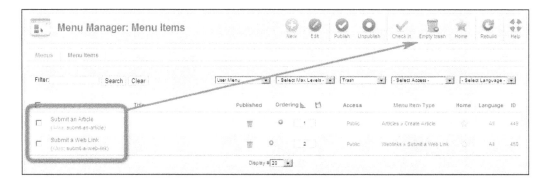

The **Empty Trash** button has the same function as the former **Delete** button in Joomla! 1.5.

Creating or editing individual Menu Items

Up to now, we've had a look at the **Menu Manager** screens and functionality. It's high time to take our exploration one step further and examine how you can edit individual menu items in Joomla! 1.6 . To create or open a menu item, go to **Menu Manager | Menu Items** and either click on **New** or click on the name (in the **Title** column) of an existing menu item. If you choose the second option, this will open a screen similar to the one shown below:

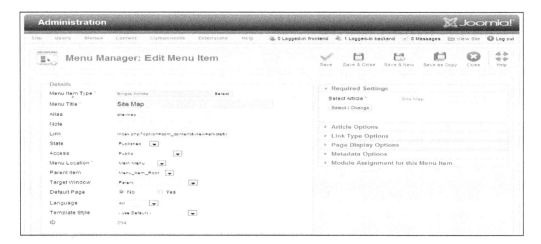

What's new? Most importantly, in the **Details** section you can choose from an updated set of Menu Item Types, and the formerly named **Parameters** on the right-hand side of the screen have changed to new sets of **Settings** and **Options**.

New toolbar buttons

In the **Edit Menu Item** (or **New Menu Item**) screen you'll recognize the new toolbar buttons that you've used in previous chapters. You can click on **Save as Copy** to save the current menu item as a copy, or you can click on **Save & New** to save the menu item and start creating a new menu item without going back to the Menu Items list.

Choosing from new Menu Item Types

When you add or edit a menu link, you're now presented with a reorganized and renamed list of menu link types. In the **Edit Menu Item** screen, go to the **Menu Item Type** field and click on the **Select** button to view the available types:

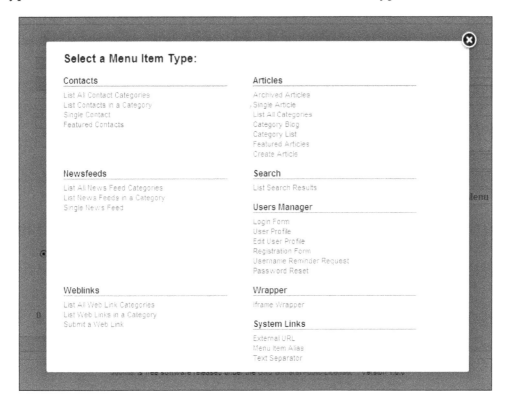

Most of these link types are the same as the ones in Joomla! 1.5; only the names have changed. As an example, let's examine the type of menu links you're likely to use most often: those in the **Articles** section. The table below shows what's changed here:

Articles menu links in 1.5:	Changed to this in 1.6:
Archive - Archived Article List	**Archived Articles**
Article - Article Layout	**Single Article**
Article - Article Submission Layout	**Create Article**
Category - Category Blog Layout	**Category Blog**
Category - Category List Layout	**Category List**
Front Page - Front Page Blog Layout	**Featured Articles**
Section - Section Blog Layout	(Replaced by **Category Blog**)
Section - Section Layout	(Replaced by **Category List**)
	(All new:) **List All Categories**

New Menu Link Item type # 1: List All Categories

The only new option in the Articles section is **List All Categories**. We've discussed this link type earlier in this book in the chapter on working with categories. Have a look at *Chapter 3* to find out how you can deploy this menu item type to create a listing of article categories.

New Menu Link Item type # 2: List All Contact Categories

Among the other link item types listed, there's one new addition in the **Contacts** section: **List All Contact Categories**. Let's find out how this can be put to use.

Exploring the use of Contact Categories in the sample site

In the Joomla! sample website, the new **List All Contact Categories** menu link is used in the Fruit Shop site. To take a look, navigate to **Sample Sites | Fruit Shop** and click on **Fruit Encyclopedia**:

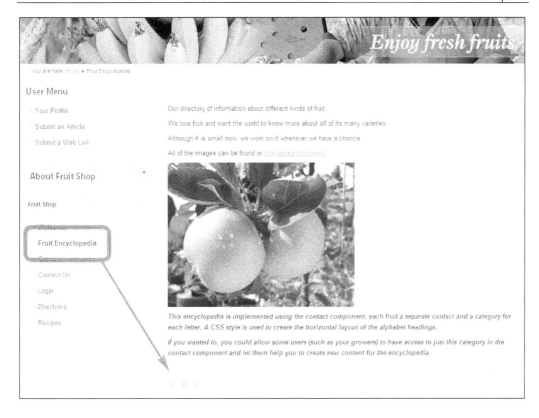

This page is the output of the new **List All Contact Categories** menu item type. The available "contact" categories shown are A, B and T.

The Fruit Encyclopedia could have been built using articles, but the developers have chosen to use the Contacts component, as this can be easily used as a database containing any type of information. Obviously, apples and bananas aren't contacts (or are they?), but the sample site does show a creative way to make use of the contact system. To understand how you can use the **List All Contact Categories** menu item type yourself, let's explore how this is set up in the backend of the sample site:

1. Go to **Components | Contacts**.

   Click on the **Categories** tab to get an overview of all the Contact Categories. As you can see, this screen resembles the article category screen; contact categories can be infinitely nested too. Child categories are displayed indented:

   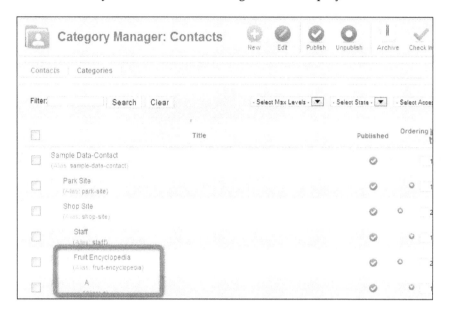

2. You can see that the **Fruit Encyclopedia** category is the parent contact category of the categories **A – Z**. Click on the **Contacts** tab to switch from the categories overview to the individual contacts assigned to these categories:

   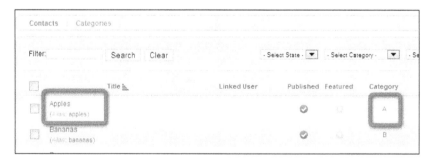

3. You'll notice that the Fruit encyclopedia is far from complete (Category **A**, for example, contains just one "contact", **Apples**). Click on the **Apples** link to see what data have been entered for this "contact" (or encyclopedia entry). You'll notice, for example, that the apple image is in fact the contact image found in the Contact Details panel.

4. Now let's find out how all this information has been made visible in the frontend. Close the **Contact Manager** and go **Menus | Fruit Shop**. In the **Menu Items** screen, a link **Fruit Encyclopedia** is shown:

5. Click on the link to view its settings. You'll notice that the **Menu Item Type** is **List All Contact Categories** and the **Top Level Category** is set to **Fruit Encyclopedia**.

That's it — this is how the Fruit Encyclopedia is set up. You can use the same principle to enter information on contacts, types of fruit, or punk bands, for that matter. In the next section, we'll see how you can do that.

Creating a database overview using the List All Contact Categories Menu Item Type

Want to create your own little database of anything? Let's find out how you can use the contacts component and the **List All Contact Categories** Menu Item Type the same way it's done in the sample data. This will give you a good idea of how you can use this powerful and highly customizable new menu item for much more than just "contacts":

1. Go to **Components | Contacts | Categories** and click on **New** to create a new category. The **Add a New Contact Category** screen opens. Enter the appropriate details of the main category. In this example, enter **Punk Band Encyclopedia** as the title and add a short description, as shown in the screenshot below:

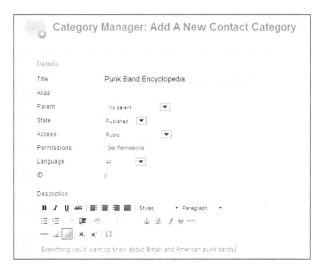

2. Click on **Save & New** to store the main category and then enter the details of the first subcategory we want to set up: enter **British Punk Bands** as the **Title**, select **Punk Band Encyclopedia** as its parent, and add a short **Description**.

3. Click on **Save & New** to enter a second subcategory called **American Punk Bands**, select **Punk Band Encyclopedia** as its parent, and add a short **Description**. You're done creating categories, so click on **Save & Close**.

4. Now create some actual encyclopedia entries: "contacts"! Go to the **Contact Manager: Contacts** screen and click on **New** to enter a new contact. Enter a name (for example **The Clash**), assign the contact to the **British Punk Bands** category, enter the encyclopedia entry text in the **Other information** box, and in the **Contact Details**, assign an image (in this example any image will do):

5. Use **Save & New** to create a set of contacts—adding other bands, their names, information, and pictures. Assign each of the contacts to one of the punk bands categories. Once done, click on **Save & Close**.You've now got a set of contacts assigned to the appropriate categories. To get these categories to display on the frontend, there's just one thing left to do: create a menu link of the **List All Contact Categories** type. Go to **Menus | Main Menu** and click on **New** to add a new menu item. In the **Details** section, select the **List All Contact Categories** menu item type. Enter a **Menu Title** (for example **Punk Band Encyclopedia**) and select **Punk Band Encyclopedia** in the **Select a Top Level Category** drop-down list:

6. Now tweak the options that determine what category information is shown when visitors click on the **Punk Band Encyclopedia** menu link. In the **Categories Options** panel, set **Top Level Category Description** to **Show**, set **Empty Categories** to **Show** and set **Subcategories Descriptions** to **Show**. In the **Category Options**, set **Category Title** to **Show**.

7. Click on **Save & Close** and then click on **View site** to see the results. A new menu link is displayed, pointing to a list of contact categories in a way similar to the sample site Fruit Encyclopedia link:

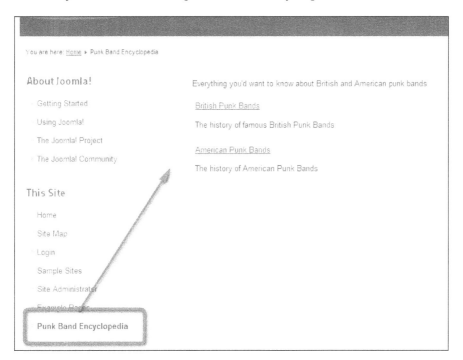

8. When visitors click on the **British Punk Bands** link (you'll probably want to try this out now), they are shown contact details in a so-called List Layout, a table of contacts in a category. If you want to customize what's shown on this list page, edit the menu link you've just created and adjust the settings in the **List Layouts** panel. Here you can hide any details (such as **Position** or **Phone**) you don't want to display in the list. In the example below, only the contact names have been set to show:

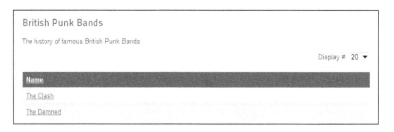

9. Clicking on the name of any band ("contact") takes the visitor to the details page. To customize what's shown on this page, adjust the **Contact Display Options** panel of the menu link you've just created. For example, by setting the **Display format** to **Plain**, all the contact information will be shown on one page, as shown in the screenshot below. On this page the contact details (Name, Image, Position, Other information) are displayed:

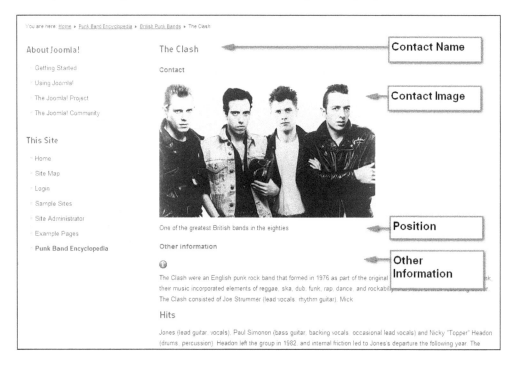

10. You might want to try and change a few other **Contact Display Options,** as there are several ways available to present the contact information. To spark your imagination, here's how the page looks when the **Display Format** in **Contact Display Options** is set to **Tabs:**

Now wait a minute! How did the heading change from **Contact** to **Photograph** in the above screenshot? You're right, I've cheated. There's no way to change these headings using the Contacts component. However, in Joomla! 1.6, you can override default language strings. In this case, the trick is to save a text file with the name `en-GB.override.ini` on the web server in the `language\en-GB\overrides` folder. (If you use another language, for example `en-US`, the path and file name change accordingly.) This `en-GB.override.ini` file contains just one line: `COM_CONTACT_DETAILS="Photograph"`. Adding this override file causes Joomla! to replace the default text for this particular heading by the text entered in the appropriate line(s).

If you want to change other strings, first find the original line in the original language file in the `language\en-GB` folder on the web server. The text file containing the language strings for the contact component is called `en-GB.com_contact.ini`. View the contents of the file in a text editor to find the lines you want to change and change your override file accordingly. To learn more about this feature, see `http://docs.joomla.org/International_Enhancements_for_ Version_1.6#Language_String_Overrides`.

Setting the template for an individual menu item

In the **Edit/New Menu Item** screen, you'll notice a new **Template Style** field. This allows you to assign a template to a specific menu item. Previously, you could assign a template to menu items only from the Template Manager. To find out more about assigning template styles, have a look at *Chapter 6* on templates.

An overview of Menu Item Options

Joomla! 1.5 menu item details featured some cryptically named Parameters. In Joomla! 1.6, these have been renamed **Options** and have been rearranged:

Joomla! 1.5 Menu Item Parameters	Joomla! 1.6 Menu Item Options
▸ Parameters (Basic)	▸ Layout Options
▸ Parameters (Advanced)	▸ Article Options
▸ Parameters (Component)	▸ Integration Options
▸ Parameters (System)	▸ Link Type Options
	▸ Page Display Options
	▸ Metadata Options
	▸ Module Assignment for this Menu Item

The exact options depend on the menu type you've selected. In the section on the List All Contacts Categories, you've seen that specific menu item types can have dozens of settings, enabling you to highly customize the menu link output. However, for many menu item types, the current sets of options will seem familiar for Joomla! 1.5 users. Let's find out how the Options panels are set up in general. As an example, let's have a closer look at the options of the **Home** menu link.

Layout Options

The first panel, **Layout Options**, contains options you'd previously find in the Parameters (Basic) and Parameters (Advanced). These options all have to do with the way information is presented and arranged on the output page:

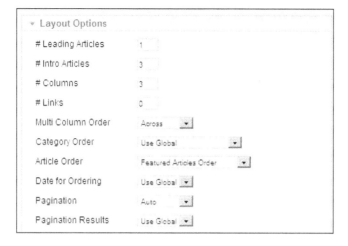

Article Options

These are the options that apply to all the articles that are displayed through this menu link. You can determine what details (Title, Author, and so on) you want to display with the articles. The Article Options are similar to the options previously found in the Parameters (Component):

Integration Options

The **Integration Options** panel is new to Joomla! 1.6, but its contents are familiar. It contains two RSS Feed options, that previously, for some strange reason, were covered separately in the Parameters (Advanced) and Parameters (Component). The **Show Feed Link option** allows you to show or hide an RSS Feed Link. This will display a feed icon in the address bar of the web browser. The **For each feed item show** option allows you to control what to show in the news feed — the intro text of each article, or the full article:

The **Link Type Options** box is new too. The **Link Title Attribute** allows you to add an optional description that will be displayed when the mouse cursor hovers over the menu hyperlink:

In the above example, we've entered dummy text (**Link Title Attribute**) here for the **Getting Started** link; in the frontend this is displayed like this:

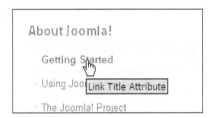

The **Link CSS Style** field allows you to apply a customized CSS style to the current menu item hyperlink. For example, if you create a class called customstyle and enter the name **customstyle** in the **Link CSS Style** box, in the HTML output of this page, the class customstyle will be applied to the current menu link:

```
<li> id="current" class="active item435">
  <a class="customstyle"
```

```
ref="/index.php?option=com_content&amp;view=featured&amp;
   Itemid=435" >Home
  </a>
</li>
```

The **Link Image** option allows you to add an image to the current menu link; this was formerly found as Menu Image in the Parameters (System). The **Add Menu Title** option is new to Joomla! 1.6 and lets you choose whether you want to display the Menu Title text next to the Menu Image. Setting this option to **No** allows you to have menu items that consist of only icons.

Page Display Options

The **Page Display Options** are shown in the screenshot below:

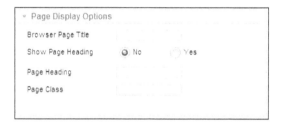

The **Page Display Options** are great for Search Engine Optimization purposes. They allow you to add a specific **Browser Page Title**. This is the text contained in the HTML `title` element, which is commonly displayed in the browser title bar. You can also enter a **Page Heading**; this is the text in the H1 element which is typically the main heading in the page content. If you don't enter anything here, Joomla! will use the menu link text as the page heading. Set **Show Page Heading** to **Yes** to make sure that the new Page Heading will be displayed on the page. In other words, Joomla! allows you to set both the `title` element and the H1 element for any menu item just as you like.

 You'll learn more about changing the **Browser Page Title** in *Chapter 8* on SEO.

The **Page Class** field allows you to enter a CSS class which will be added to the CSS class defining the content area of this page. For example, the main content of the **Getting Started** page in the sample content is contained in a DIV element which by default has the CSS class `item-page` applied to it. When you enter **customclass** in the **Page Class** field, this CSS class will be changed to `item-pagecustomclass`. By creating specific CSS classes, you can apply specific styling to the pages the current menu link points to.

Metadata Options

The **Metadata Options** are new to Joomla! 1.6. These are important for Search
Engine Optimization purposes and allow you to enter metadata for the pages
that the current menu link points to. You can add a description, meta keywords
and enter instructions for robots (web search engine spiders):

To learn more about robots and what to enter here, have a look at
`http://www.robotstxt.org/robotstxt.html`.

Module Assignment for this Menu Item

The **Module Assignment for this Menu Item** box is a really clever addition.
It displays links to all the modules assigned to the current item:

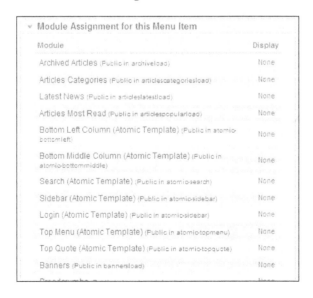

Just as in Joomla! 1.5, modules are always assigned to one or more menu items. However, in the Joomla! backend, menus and modules were always dealt with separately. In Joomla! 1.6, menus and modules are more closely integrated.

In the sample site, this box contains a very long list, as this list includes *all* modules, not just those assigned to the menu item. The idea is that you can assign or edit any module right from the menu item settings.

Changing the module settings from the menu item

Let's try out the new possibilities of the Menu Item edit screen and change module settings right from this screen. Let's say we've decided that we want to change the display of one of the modules in the sample site, the **Who's online** module. We want to make this module appear on the home page of our site. To do this, we first open the **Home** menu item settings and select the appropriate module right there:

1. Go to **Menu Manager | Menus** and click on the **Main Menu** name in the **Title** column:

2. In the **Menu Items** list, click on the **Home** link to edit it:

3. In the **Edit Menu Item** screen, click on the **Module Assignment for this Menu Item** link to reveal links to all modules:

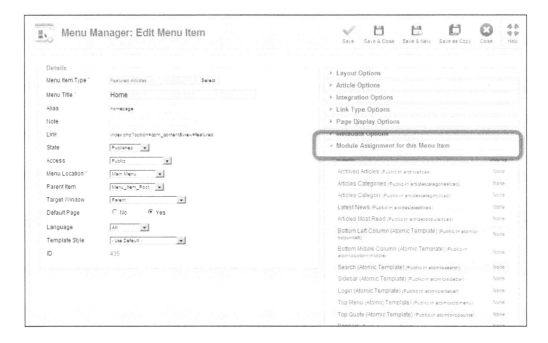

4. Scroll down the list to find the **Who's Online** module. Click on the module name to edit its settings:

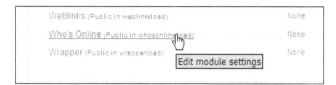

5. The module **Position** is currently set to **whosonlineload**. This means that it's being called from within an article in the sample data; it will only display within that single article. We've decided that we want to change this. We want to display the **Who's Online** module in the left column. To do this, select **Position**: **position-7**.

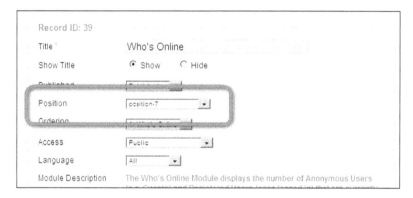

6. We also want the **Who's Online** module to display only on the home page. In the **Menu Assignment** section, scroll down to find the Main Menu **Home** link. Tick its select box:

7. Click on **Save & Close** to close the pop up window and return to the **Edit Menu Item** screen. Click on **Save & Close** to close this screen and then click on **View Site** to see the output on the frontend. The module is now shown on the home page in the left-hand side column:

Summary

In this chapter, we've covered many improvements in the way you deal with menus and menu items in Joomla! 1.6:

- The **Menu Manager** features two tabbed screens: **Menus** and **Menu Items**. The **Menu Manager: Menus** screen offers you a number of shortcuts to get straight to the set of menu items you want to check or edit.

- You can jump straight from the **Menu Manager** to the appropriate menu module to change its settings. No more clicking back and forth between Menu Manager and Module Manager!

- The **Menu Manager: Menu Items** screen allows you to access the desired set of menu items through a range of filtering options.

- At the bottom of the **Menu Items** screen, a new section called **Batch process the selected menu items** allows you to move, copy, or set the access level of selected menu items all at once.

- When you add or edit a menu link, you're now presented with an updated list of Menu Link Item types. Two new items are the **List All Categories** menu link and the **List All Contact Categories** menu link.

- Joomla! 1.5 menu item Parameters have been renamed **Options** and they have been rearranged.

- In Joomla! 1.6, you can only assign modules directly to menu items, without having to go to the Module Manager first. Through the menu link settings (in the new **Module Assignment for this Menu Item** panel) you determine what modules display when visitors click on this menu link.

In the first four chapters, you've learned about the improvements in Joomla's core capabilities: managing content, menus, and modules. In the next chapter, we'll plunge into a more advanced topic: controlling user access.

5
Managing Site Users with Access Control

One of the biggest changes in Joomla! 1.6 is the introduction of a completely new system to manage user permissions. The previous version of Joomla! already featured a basic system of Access Control Levels (ACL), as user permissions management is usually called. In Joomla! 1.6, you've got much more control over what users can see and do on the site. However, the new system can be pretty complex. Let's find out how you can put Joomla!'s new ACL system to work.

In this chapter, you'll learn about:

- The default set of user groups and permissions in Joomla! 1.6
- Action Permissions: what users can do
- Viewing Access Levels: what users can see
- ACL at work: two practical examples of how you can use ACL

What's new about the Access Control Levels system?

In Joomla! 1.5, a fixed set of user groups was available, ranging from "Public" users (anyone with access to the frontend of the site) to "Super Administrators", allowed to log in to the backend and do anything. The ACL system in Joomla! 1.6 is much more flexible:

- Instead of fixed user groups with fixed sets of permissions, you can create as many groups as you want and grant the people in those groups any combination of permissions. ACL enables you to control anything users can do on the site: log in, create, edit, delete, publish, unpublish, trash, archive, manage, or administer things.

- Users are no longer limited to only one group: a user can belong to different groups at the same time. This allows you to give particular users both the set of permissions for one group and another group without having to create a third, combined set of permissions from the ground up.

- Permissions no longer apply to the whole site as they did in Joomla! 1.5. You can now set permissions for specific parts of the site. Permissions apply to either the whole site, or to specific components, categories, or items (such as a single article).

What are the default user groups and permissions?

The flexibility of the new ACL system has a downside: it can also get quite complex. The power to create as many user groups as you like, each with very fine-grained sets of permissions assigned to them, means you can easily get entangled in a web of user groups, Joomla! Objects, and permissions.

You should carefully plan the combinations of permissions you need to assign to different user groups. Before you change anything in Joomla!, sketch an outline or use mind mapping tools (such as http://bubbl.us) to get an overview of what you want to accomplish through Joomla! ACL: who (which users) should be able to see or do what in which parts of the site?

In many cases, you might not need to go beyond the default setup and just use the default users groups and permissions that are already present when you install Joomla! 1.6. So, before we go and find out how you can craft custom user groups and their distinctive sets of permissions, let's have a look at the default Joomla! 1.6 ACL setup.

The default site-wide settings

In broad terms, the default groups and permissions present in Joomla! 1.6 are much like the ACL system that was available in Joomla! 1.5. To view the default groups and their permissions, go to **Site | Global Configuration | Permissions**. The **Permission Settings** screen is displayed, showing a list of User Groups. A user group is a collection of users sharing the same permissions, such as **Public**, **Manager**, or **Administrator**.

By default the permission settings of the **Public** user group are shown; clicking any of the other user group names reveals the settings for that particular group.

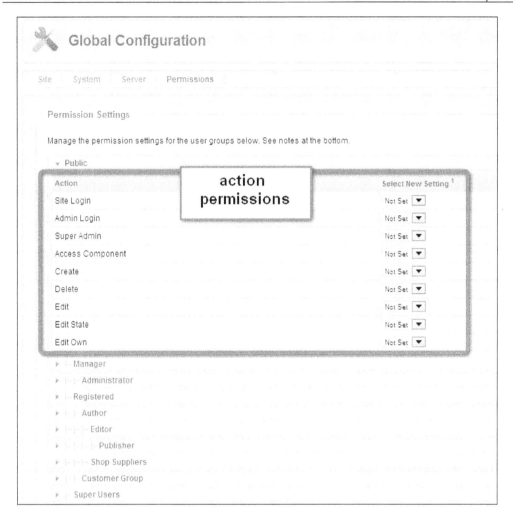

On the right-hand side of the **Permission Settings** screen, the generic (site-wide) action permissions for this group are displayed: **Site Login**, **Admin Login**, and so on. **Actions** are the things users are allowed do on the site. For the sample user groups, these action permissions have already been set.

What are Action Permissions?

Site Login, **Admin Login**, **Super Admin** ... the new permissions in Joomla! 1.6 have somewhat cryptic names. To understand what they mean, see Action permissions: what users can do further in this chapter.

Default user groups

Let's find out what these default user groups are about. We'll discuss the user groups from the most basic level (**Public**) to the most powerful (**Super Users**).

Public – the guest group

This is the most basic level; anyone visiting your site is considered part of the Public group. Members of the Public group can view the frontend of the site, but they don't have any special permissions.

Registered – the user group that can log in

Registered users are regular site visitors, except for the fact that they are allowed to log in to the frontend of the site. After they have logged in with their account details, they can view content that may be hidden from ordinary site visitors because the **Access** level of that content has been set to **Registered**. This way, Registered users can be presented all kinds of content ordinary (Public) users can't see.

Registered users, however, can't contribute content. They're part of the user community, not web team.

Author, Editor, Publisher – the frontend content team

Authors, Editors, and Publishers are allowed to log in to the frontend, to edit or add articles. There are three types of frontend content contributors, each with their specific permission levels:

- Authors can create new content for approval by a Publisher or someone higher in rank. They can edit their own articles, but can't edit existing articles created by others.
- Editors can create new articles and edit existing articles. A Publisher or higher must approve their submissions.
- Publishers can create, edit, and publish, unpublish, or trash articles in the frontend. They cannot delete content.

Manager, Administrator, Super User – the backend administrators

Managers, Administrators and Super Users are allowed to log in to the backend to add and manage content and to perform administrative tasks.

- **Managers** can do all that Publishers can, but they are also allowed to log in to the backend of the site to create, edit, or delete articles. They can also create and manage categories. They have limited access to administration functions.

- **Administrators** can do all that Managers can and have access to more administration functions. They can manage users, edit, or configure extensions and change the site template. They can use manager screens (User Manager, Article Manager, and so on) and can create, delete, edit, and change the state of users, articles, and so on.

- **Super Users** can do everything possible in the backend. (In Joomla! 1.5, this user group type was called Super Administrator). When Joomla! is installed, there's always one Super User account created. That's usually the person who builds and customizes the website. In the current example website, you're the Super User.

Shop Suppliers and Customers – two sample user groups

You'll notice two groups in the **Permission Settings** screen that we haven't covered yet: **Shop Suppliers** and **Customer**. These are added when you install the Joomla! 1.6 sample data. These aren't default user groups; they are used in the sample Fruit Shop site to show how you can create customized groups.

Are there also sample users available?

As there are user groups present in the sample data, you might expect there are also sample users. This is not the case. There are no (sample) users assigned to the sample user groups. There's just one user available after you've installed Joomla! – you. You can view your details by navigating to **Users | User Manager**. You're taken to the **User Manager: Users** screen:

Here you can see that your name is Super User, your user name is admin (unless you've changed this yourself when setting up your account), and you're part of the user group called Super Users.

 There's also a shortcut available to take you to your own basic user settings: click on **Site | My Profile** or – even faster – just click on the **Edit Profile** shortcut in the Control Panel. However, you can't manage user permissions here; the purpose of the **My Profile** screen is only to manage basic user settings.

Action Permissions: what users can do

We've now seen what types of users are present in the default setup of Joomla! 1.6. The action permissions that you can grant these user groups – things they can *do* on the site – are shown per user group in the **Site | Global Configuration | Permissions** screen. Click on any of the user group names to see the permission settings for that group:

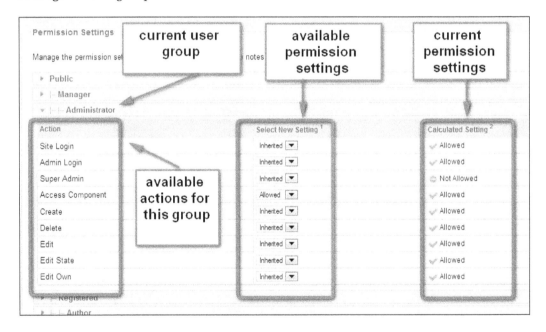

You'll also find these permissions (such as **Site Login, Create, Delete, Edit**) on other places in the Joomla! interface: after all, you don't just apply permissions on a site-wide basis (as you could in previous versions of Joomla!), but also on the level of components, categories, or individual items.

To allow or deny users to do things, each of the available actions can be set to **Allowed** or **Denied** for a specific user group. If the permission for an action isn't explicitly allowed or denied, it is **Not Set**.

Permissions are inherited

You don't have to set each and every permission on every level manually: permissions are *inherited* between groups. That is, a child user group automatically gets the permissions set for its parent.

Wait a minute—parents, children, inheritance ... how does that work? To understand these relationships, let's have a look at the overview of user groups in the **Permission Settings** screen. This shows all available user groups (I've edited this screen image a little to be able to show all the user groups in one column):

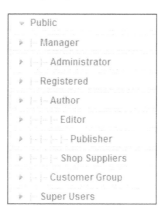

You'll notice that all user group names are displayed indented, apart from **Public**. This indicates the permissions hierarchy: **Public** is the parent group, **Manager** (indented one position) is a child of **Public**, **Administrator** (indented two positions) is a child of **Manager**.

Permissions for a parent group are automatically inherited by all child groups (unless these permissions are explicitly set to **Allowed** or **Denied** to "break" the inheritance relationship). In other words: a child group can do anything a parent group can do—and more, as it is a child and therefore has its own specific permissions set.

For example, as Authors are children of the Registered group, they inherit the permissions of the Registered group (that is, the permission to log in to the frontend of the site). Apart from that, Authors have their own specific permissions added to the permissions of the Registered group.

> Setting an action to **Denied** is very powerful: you can't allow an action for a lower level in the permission hierarchy if it is set to Denied higher up in the hierarchy. So, if an action is set to Denied for a higher group, this action will be inherited all the way down the permissions "tree" and will always be denied for all lower levels — even if you explicitly set the lower level to **Allowed**.

What do the available action permissions mean?

In the **Site | Global Configuration | Permissions** screen, nine types of action permissions are available, such as **Site Login** and **Admin login**. However, the available action permissions vary through the different levels of the site for which you can set permissions. You can set action permissions at up to four levels on the website, ranging from site-wide permissions to permissions on the level of individual items, such as articles. Let's have a look at the possibilities: the different action permissions you can set on different levels.

Level 1 – site-wide permissions in Global Configuration

You can set the default permissions for each action and group site-wide, via **Site | Global Configuration | Permissions**:

The table below explains what the available permissions in **Global Configuration** mean:

Permission name	Allows user to do the following
Site Login	Log in to the front of the website.
Admin Login	Log in to the backend administration interface.
Super Admin	Do anything on the site, including Global Configuration (Super Users have Super Admin rights).
Access Component	Have administrative access to components, but not to Global Configuration.
Create	Create new content in components.
Delete	Delete content in components.

Permission name	Allows user to do the following
Edit	Edit content in components.
Edit State	Change the state (publish, unpublish, trash, archive) of content in components.
Edit Own	Edit content they've created themselves.

The Super Admin action is only available in the Global Configuration Permissions screen, as it applies only to the whole site.

Level 2 – permissions for components

You can set permissions on the level of components. Joomla! components are Articles, Menus, Users, Banners, and so on. There's a **Permissions** screen in each of the components of Joomla! 1.6. For example, go to **Article Manager | Options | Permissions** to access the **Permissions** screen of the Article Manager:

Other component permissions screens can be found in a similar way through the **Options** button: for example, navigate to **Menus | Menu Manager** and click on **Options** to access the article permissions, or go to **Components | Banners** and click on **Options | Permissions** to access permission settings for the banner component.

You'll notice that there's one action in the list that we haven't seen yet, **Configure**. It's only applicable to components. The table below explains what the available action permissions for components mean:

Permission name	Allows user to do the following
Configure	Set component options.
Access Component	Have administrative access to component.
Create	Create content in component.
Delete	Delete content in component.
Edit	Edit content in component.
Edit State	Change the state (publish, unpublish, trash, archive) of content in component.
Edit Own	Edit content that they've created themselves.

Level 3 – permissions for categories

You can also set permissions on the level of specific categories. In the screen where you create or edit a category (such as **Content | Category Manager | Edit** or **New**), you'll find a **Category Permissions** section at the bottom of the screen:

In this section, you can set permissions for all articles within a specific category. The **Calculated Setting** column on the right-hand side displays whether the specific action is **Allowed** or **Not Allowed**; in the **Select New Setting** drop-down box, you can change the current values.

In the same way, you can set permissions for types of categories other than Article Categories, such as Contacts categories or Banners categories.

The table below explains what the available action permissions for categories mean:

Permission name	Allows user to do the following
Create	Create content and subcategories in category.
Delete	Delete category, subcategories, and category content.
Edit	Edit category, subcategories, and category content.
Edit State	Change the state (publish, unpublish, trash, archive) of category, subcategories, and category content.
Edit Own	Edit their own category, subcategories, and category content.

Level 4 – permissions for articles

Finally, you can set permissions on the level of individual articles. As an example, go to **Content | Article Manager | Edit** or **New** to set permissions for a specific article in the **Article Permissions** section at the bottom of the screen:

The table below explains what the available action permissions for articles mean

Permission name	Allows user to do the following
Delete	Delete article.
Edit	Edit article.
Edit State	Change the state (publish, unpublish, trash, archive) of article.

Viewing Access Levels: what users can see

We've now covered two main parts of the ACL system: User Groups and action permissions (the specific things users can be allowed to do). A third important ACL concept is Viewing Access Levels. These access levels don't determine what users can do, but what users can see: can users only see the public site, can they access the frontend or maybe access the backend? What articles, menus, modules, or components can the user group actually view?

By default, three Viewing Access Levels are available: **Public**, **Registered**, and **Special**. Go to **Users | User Manager** and click on the **Viewing Access Levels** tab to see these levels:

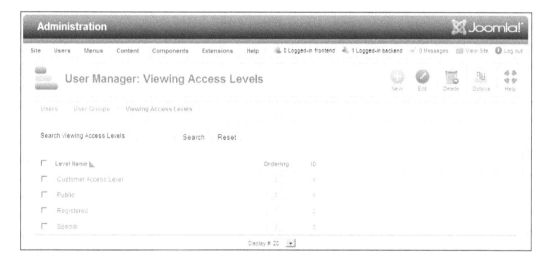

This is what the three default Viewing Access Levels mean:

- **Public** means that there are no special viewing permissions involved. It's the set of permissions for the Public user group, who are only allowed access to the public site.

- **Registered** is the set of permissions for Registered Users. These by default are allowed to log in to the site to view the site parts that are set to the Registered access level.

- **Special** is the set of viewing permissions for all users that can log in to the backend (Manager, Administrator, Super User).

At the top of the list, there's an extra viewing level: **Customer Access Level**. This is an example of customized access levels available in the sample data. It's used in the Fruit Shop sample site.

Viewing Access Levels can be set for all kinds of content on the site, from modules and menu items to individual articles, by changing the value of the Access drop-down list:

When the **Access** value of an article or another object is set to **Registered**, **Special**, or any other level that's not **Public**, this content will only be visible for user groups who have that particular Viewing Access Level assigned.

Wrapping up: the ingredients of ACL

Applying ACL is all about combining the concepts we've covered up to now: creating a User Group and setting Viewing Access Levels and Action Permissions for (specific levels of) your site. In the rest of this chapter, we'll explore a few real life examples to find out how this works.

ACL at work: how to control user permissions

Setting permissions involves the following three steps:

1. Create a user group (a group of people sharing the same permissions).

2. Tell Joomla! what the group can see or do. In other words, you assign a viewing access level and set the action permissions for this user group.

3. Add users to the group.

Let's find out how you can set permissions using this three-step approach. First, we'll open up the backend of the sample site for site designers: users who can only access and do things in the **Template Manager**. After that, we'll create a user group that's allowed to update the **Events** page on the site.

ACL example 1: allow specific users to manage contacts

Let's assume that you need a new type of user: someone who's able to administer the contacts database of your site, accessed through **Components | Contacts**. On the site you're building, the contacts database contains the names and contact details of all employees. You want to allow the company secretaries to manage and update contact details, but you don't want them to be able to access anything other than that. Let's find out how to achieve this.

Step 1: create a user group

1. Go to **Users | Groups** and click on **New** to create a new group called **Contacts Administrator**, as shown below. Set the **Group Parent** to **Registered**. This way, the group gets the Login permission from the Registered group, but no other permissions:

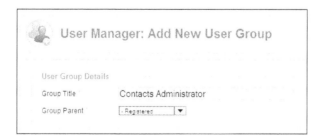

2. Click on **Save & Close** to save the group that you've just created.

Step 2: tell Joomla! what the group can see and do

To specify what the (future) members of the new user group can see and do, we'll first specify which viewing access level this user group has. In this case, we want the new user group to be able to access the backend. For this, we can use an existing viewing access level: the **Special** Access Level, one of the default permission levels, which has the desired viewing access levels assigned to it. Anyone with **Special** level can access the backend controls:

1. Go to **Users | Access Levels**. The existing **Viewing Access Levels** are shown:

2. To add the new user group to the **Special** Access Level, click on the Level Name **Special.** Add the new **Contacts Administrator** user group to this level by clicking on the select box to the left of the name **Contacts Administrator**:

3. Click on **Save & Close** to save your changes.

So far, you've created a user group and made it possible for its users to view the backend once they've logged in, by assigning them to the **Special** level. However, they still can't actually log in to the backend. Logging in to the backend is an action—and that specific action permission is set through the **Admin Login** permission in the **Global Configuration**. Let's fix this now and give the Contacts Administrator permission to access the backend:

4. Go to **Site | Global Configuration | Permissions**. Click on the **Contacts Administrator** user group name. The permissions panel for this group opens.

5. For this group, change the **Admin Login** permission to **Allowed**:

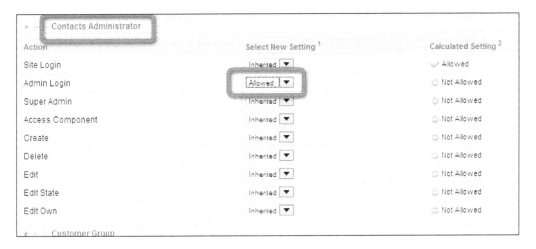

6. Click on **Save & Close**.

Secondly, we have to set permissions for our new group to manage contacts in the backend. We need to set this permission at the level of the Contacts component:

7. Go to Components | Contacts and click on the **Options** button.

8. Click on the **Permissions** tab to change the permissions to **Allowed** for this group for any action, as shown below:

9. Click on **Save & Close** to commit the changes.

Setting permissions is done. Users in this group can now access the backend and manage contacts, but they won't be able to do anything else. However, as yet there are no members assigned to this group. One last thing to take care of!

Step 3: add users to the group

Let's create one user who is a member of the Contacts Administrator group.

1. Go to **Users | User Manager** and click on **Add new user**. Enter the required details: **Name**, **Login Name**, **Password**, and **E-mail**.

2. In the **Assigned User Groups** section, assign the new user to the appropriate Action Permissions group by ticking the box to the left of the **Contacts Administrator** group name:

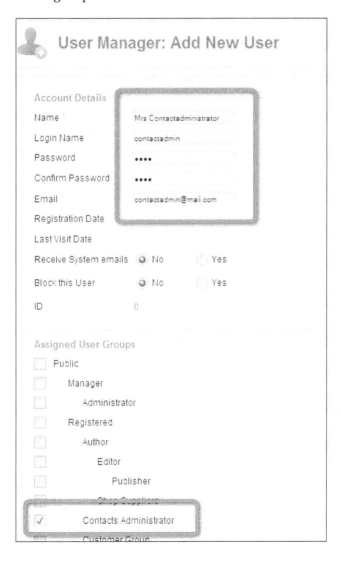

3. Click on **Save & Close** to save your changes.

Check if it works

To find out if everything is set up correctly, log out and log in to the backend as the new user. You'll notice that the backend interface is almost empty. Most of the usual menus and shortcuts have disappeared or are dysfunctional. Only the functions relevant to the new user group are available; the only component that the user can see and access is **Contacts**:

Click on the **Components | Contacts | Contacts** submenu link. You'll notice that all the functionality related to managing contacts is available for the new user:

ACL example 2: allow users to edit one specific article

In the previous example, you made one component (Joomla!'s contact management functionality) available to one specific user group. Let's now find out how we can set permissions for the very basic content level: *one article*. Imagine a club website with an Events Calendar page: an article listing club events. Wouldn't it be great if that list could be updated by members of the committee that organizes these events?

Let's create an account for specific club members who can log in to the front end, open the specific article, edit it, and save the changes. We don't want them to be able to edit any other items on the site.

Step 1: create a user group

We'll go about this in the same order as you've seen in the first example. First, log in as Super User and create a user group for this specific task:

1. Go to **Users | Groups** and click on the **Add New Group** link to create a new user group:

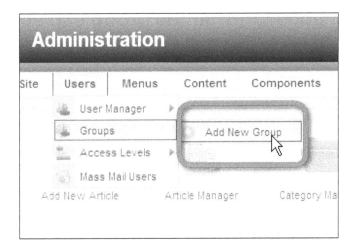

2. In the **Add New Action Permission Group** screen, enter **Calendar Updater** in the **Group Title** field. In the **Group Parent** select box, select **Registered**. This means that the new user group will inherit all the permissions of this group. As registered users are allowed to log into the site, this means that the Calendar Updaters will also be permitted to do this:

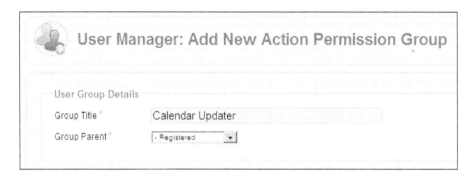

3. Click on **Save & Close**. The new group has been created. Up to now, Calendar Updaters can't do anything, except log in to the frontend.

Step 2: tell Joomla! what the group can see and do

You haven't actually assigned any permissions to this level. (The only thing you've indicated is that the new user group has the same basic permissions as the Registered group; that is, they can log in to the frontend).

Let's tell Joomla! what the permissions of this new user group are. In this case we'll set up permissions on the lowest possible content level — for one single article:

1. Go to **Content | Article Manager** and create a new article. In the **Title** field, enter **Events Calendar**. For now, you can leave this article **Uncategorised**. The **Access** value should be **Public**: after all, you want every site visitor to be able to view the article. Select **Featured: Yes** to have the article display on the homepage. In the **Article Text** editor section, enter some dummy text. The screen should look like this:

2. Click on the **Set Permissions** button to jump to the **Article Permissions** box at the bottom of the screen). Here the current article permissions are displayed. Click on the **Calendar Updater** group name. You'll notice that all possible actions are **Not Allowed** for the **Calendar Updater** group:

3. To change the permissions, in the **Select New Setting** column, change the value in the **Edit** drop-down box to **Allowed**. Click on **Save** to update the corresponding value in the **Calculated Setting** column. This will now change to **Allowed**:

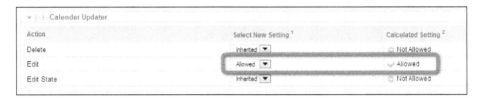

You don't have to change any other values. After all, you don't want users to be able to delete the article or to change its State (that is archive it, trash it, or unpublish it).

4. Click on **Save & Close** to commit the changes and close the article screen.

Step 3: add users to the group

The final step is adding a user and giving this new user the permissions of a Calendar Updater:

1. Go to **Users | User Manager | Add new User**.

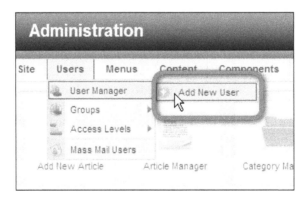

2. In the **Add New User** screen, enter the user details. In this example, we'll fill in the screen as follows:
    ◦ **Name**: John Calendar
    ◦ **Username**: john
    ◦ **Password, Confirm Password**: enter and re-type a password
    ◦ **E-mail**: enter an e-mail address

3. In the **Assigned User Groups**, make sure to select the **Calendar Updater** group name. The screen should look like this:

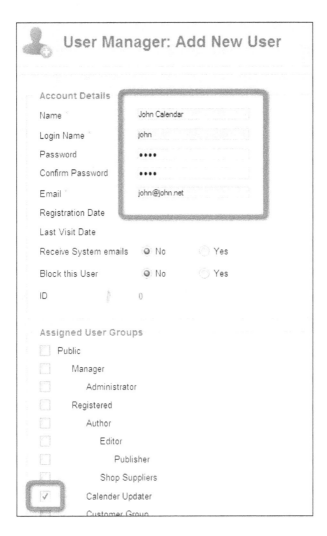

4. Click on **Save & Close** to save your changes.

Check if it works

Let's check if your settings have the desired effects. Let's log in to the frontend as the new user we've just created:

1. Go to the frontend. On the home page **Login Form**, log in with the **User Name** and **Password** you've created:

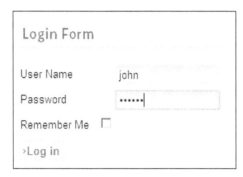

2. Click on the **Calender** article on the home page. To see the Calendar article, you may have to click on the **Next** link below the home page articles: due to the default home page settings, the article you've added will be displayed on the second page.

    You'll notice that an icon is displayed to the right of the **Calendar** article title, indicating that you can edit the article:

3. Click on the icon to open the frontend article **Editor** screen that allows you to edit the article contents and save the changes:

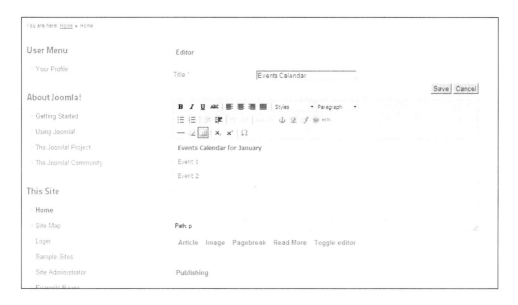

That's it. You're now able to log in as a member of the Calendar Updater user group and edit one specific article from the frontend of the website.

Allowing access to categories

In this example, we've allowed users to edit just one article. In practice, you'll often want users to edit one or more categories. This way, the web team responsible for the content of one department can be granted access to only the web pages of their department.

More on Access Control

Using ACL gives site administrators exciting new possibilities, and although the process isn't straightforward, the overview in this chapter should get you started. There's also a growing number of resources on this subject on the Web. Keep an eye on the documentation found at http://www.joomla.org (for example, have a look at http://docs.joomla.org/ACL_Tutorial_for_Joomla_1.6). However, always check if the information is up-to-date, as some ACL specifics (permission names, default permissions) have changed through the different development stages of Joomla! 1.6.

Summary

In this chapter, we've explored the exciting new possibilities of the Joomla! ACL system. This is what we have covered:

- In the User Manager, you can create new users and assign them to a specific Group, granting them various levels of access to the site.

- The default User Groups consist of seven levels, from guests (Public) to the most powerful (Super Users). These user levels are comparable to the ones present in Joomla! 1.5. However, you can now add as many custom user groups as you like.

- The permissions that you can grant these user groups — things they can do on the site — are called Action Permissions. You can set these permissions (such as **Site Login**, **Create**, **Delete**, **Edit**) on different levels in the Joomla! interface: site-wide, for components, for categories, or for individual items.

- Viewing Access Levels don't determine what users can do, but what users can see or access. By default, three Viewing Access Levels are available: **Public**, **Registered**, and **Special**, but you can create new custom levels for your specific user groups and their permissions.

- Applying ACL to control user permissions means telling Joomla! what parts of the site specific users can view and what they can do there. Setting permissions involves three steps: create a user group, tell Joomla! what the group can see or do (assign viewing access levels and action permissions), and finally add users to the group.

6
New Flexibility in Using Templates

In Joomla! 1.6, using templates is more powerful than ever before. The new Template Manager interface contains more functionality and Joomla! now comes with a set of new, great looking, and flexible templates. The built-in template options allow site administrators to customize the template styling, without having to touch HTML or CSS code. A new feature is Template Styles, allowing you to apply different versions of the same template to specific areas of the site.

In this chapter, you'll learn:

- What's new about the templates included with Joomla! 1.6
- Working with the new tabbed Template Manager
- Using Template Styles: assigning template variations to specific pages
- Exploring, editing, and customizing templates

What's new? Finally, table-less templates

Compared to previous versions, Joomla! 1.6 templates now output cleaner code. Up to version 1.5, by default, Joomla! used a notoriously outdated method to display content, deploying HTML tables not just (as intended) to display tabular data, but for page layout purposes. It was only possible to get Joomla! to output clean code using so-called template overrides. These days, table-less layout is considered a much better, more flexible way to design websites. Luckily, Joomla! 1.6 is fully up to standards in this respect.

Web standards are specifications created by the World Wide Web Consortium (W3C), led by Tim Berners-Lee, the inventor of the web. Sites using clean, semantically correct code without browser-specific hacks load faster and can be accessed more easily through different devices and browsers, including screen readers. To find out more about web standards, have a look at `http://www.webstandards.org/learn/faq`. You can also find a good introduction to the subject of web standards at `http://en.wikipedia.org/wiki/Web_standards`.

What does that clean output look like?

Want to find out what clean code looks like? Just take a peek under the hood. You can do this by selecting the **View Page Source** option in your browser.

If you are using the Firefox browser, the Firebug extension allows you to inspect both HTML and CSS code using a split browser screen: in the top screen half, the website is displayed, and in the bottom half the relevant code is shown.

 See http://getfirebug.com/whatisfirebug to find out more about downloading and using the Firebug web development extension for Firefox.

The screenshot below shows such a split screen for a page from the Joomla! 1.6 sample site, using the new default template of Joomla! 1.6, called Beez 2.0. If you're familiar with HTML, you'll notice that there's no sign of any table codes; all sections of the page layout are formatted using so-called DIV elements. Moreover, all heading elements—previously styled with proprietary Joomla! style names, such as `contentheading`—are now outputted according to web standards, using the H1 (Heading 1) style for the main title, H2 for secondary titles, and so forth.

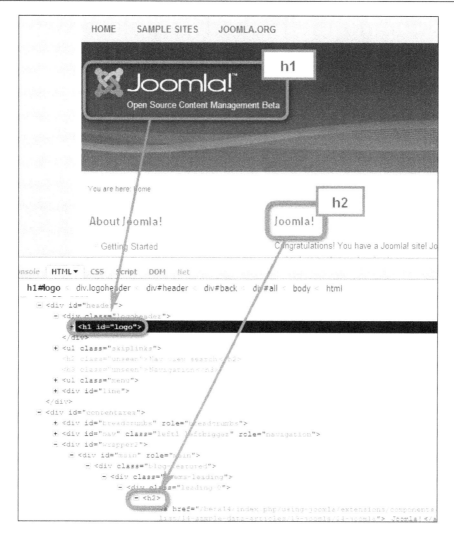

Why clean code is good for everybody

The average end user—the site visitor—probably won't notice the changes under the hood, but they're important nevertheless. It will allow people using different browsers, and different devices (ranging from smartphones to screen readers) to easily access the website. Moreover, sites with clean code will load faster and can be interpreted and indexed by search engines more easily.

Joomla!'s new coding is also a good thing if you want to design a template or customize an existing one. It's much easier to understand well-structured, meaningful markup and readable CSS class names and adapt them to your needs.

Introducing the tabbed Template Manager

You've already seen them throughout the new Joomla! backend: tabbed screens. The new tabbed Template Manager allows you to jump from the **Styles** tab to the **Templates** tab. Let's find out what those screens have to offer you.

The Styles tab: selecting templates and settings

The main purpose of the **Styles** screen is to allow you to select which of the available templates you want to use. As you can see, the current default frontend template is called Beez 2.0 (referred to as **Beez2** in this screen). The default backend template is called Bluestork:

Selecting a template

To change the default template, select the desired template and click on **Make Default**. To assign a template to the backend, select any of the Administrator templates and click on **Make Default**. In the **Assigned** column, you can see whether a template is in use (even if it isn't the default one), because it's assigned to one or more menu items.

Template Styles

The name of the **Styles** screen may cause a little confusion: you might expect that this screen enables you to change CSS styles and stylesheets that control the template design. This is not the case: a Template Style is a variation that you can create based on an existing template. In Joomla! 1.5, template designers could already add extra options to their templates, such as the option to select a template color scheme. Joomla! 1.6 adds more power to these built-in template options by allowing you to save a combination of "a template including its settings" as a Template Style. You can then assign this Template Style to one or more menu items. In other words, styles allow you to have individually styled pages or sets of pages.

One example of this is that you can make the home page display using a "green" color scheme (the first Template Style) and other pages in a "blue" color scheme (the second Template Style). We'll have a look at working with Template Styles in the section *Customizing templates using Template Styles*.

The two meanings of the word default

In the **Styles** screen, the word default is used with two different meanings. In the top button bar, the button **Make Default** works as you would expect: it allows you to make the selected template the default one for either the frontend or the backend. However, you'll also notice templates named **Default**, such as **Atomic – Default** and **Beez2 – Default**. In this case, default means it's the template using its normal settings (in other words: its default, unchanged Template Style). This is to distinguish default templates from templates with a specific style applied, such as **Beez2 – Parks Site**. The latter template is based upon the Beez2 template, but it's saved separately as a specific Template Style for the Parks Site.

The Templates tab: exploring templates and editing code

Clicking on the **Templates** tab takes you to the **Templates Manager: Templates** screen. This allows you to explore installed templates and preview them. Moreover, clicking on the template **Details** link (such as **Hathor Details**) allows you to access the template HTML and CSS files and edit template code:

Let's find out what's new in the way you'll work with templates in Joomla! 1.6. First, we'll use the Template Styles feature; later in this chapter, we'll find out how to explore and edit templates via the **Templates** screen.

Customizing templates using Template Styles

Templates can include all sorts of options, allowing the site administrator to change the template width, colors, column layout, and much more without touching a single line of HTML or CSS code. Let's find out what the main options of the new default template are and how they affect the look and feel of the template.

This new template also has some powerful options built-in. Later, we'll find out how to save these options and create template styles to apply different template variations in different parts of the site.

Changing the site color and layout options

We'll first have a look at some settings that affect the overall color scheme and the layout:

1. Navigate to **Extensions | Template Manager**. The **Template Manager: Styles** screen is displayed.

2. In the list of available templates, click on **Beez2 – Default**:

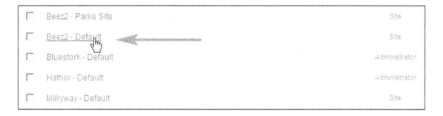

3. You're taken to the **Edit Style** screen. In the **Advanced Options** panel, the available template options are displayed:

Let's find out what the effects are of the different settings. The **Template colour** option allows for some quite powerful changes in the look and feel of the site. We'll try out the available color schemes:

4. The current template color scheme is called **Personal**. In the **Template colour** drop-down box, change this to **Nature**. Click on **Save** and then click on **View Site** to see the output:

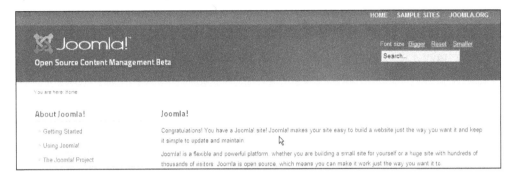

You may recognize this style from the National Parks sample site, which also has the same (dark green) Nature color scheme applied. The **Template colour** setting changes not just the main colors of the site; there are also a few changes in the layout. For example, the grey margins on the left-hand side and the right-hand site of the default design have disappeared. Moreover, the site header has a different (more neutral) background image applied and it is now displayed over the full width of the screen.

5. In the **Template Styles** screen, reverse your changes. In the **Template colour** drop-down box, select the default value: **Personal**.

6. Finally, let's find out what the effects are of the **Position of navigation** setting. Select **after content**, click on **Save,** and then click on **View Site**. You'll notice that the menu column is now placed on the right-hand side of the screen:

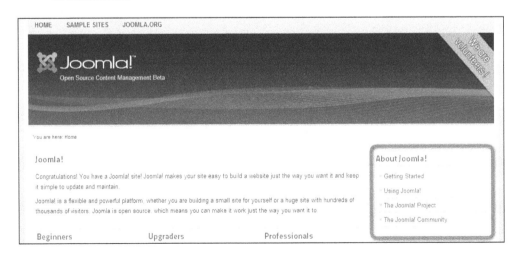

You might want to experiment with the other **Advanced Options**. The **Wrapper Small** (%) and **Wrapper Large** (%) settings allow you to change the width of the main content areas in the template. In the next section, we'll use the **Logo** option to change the site header.

Customizing the site logo

It's probably one of the first things people new to Joomla! do: changing the logo to put their mark on the site they've just started to build. In previous versions of Joomla!, you had to edit the CSS source code yourself to get rid of the default Joomla! logo. The new Beez 2 default template makes it easier to change the site logo. You can customize the logo just by changing the **Template Style** settings. Let's find out how this works:

1. Navigate to **Extensions | Template Manager**. Click on the **Styles** tab and then click on the link **Beez2 - Default**. The **Template Manager: Edit Style** screen is displayed.

2. In the **Advanced Options** panel, locate the **Logo** option and click on **Select**.

3. A pop-up screen appears. In the **Upload files** section, click on **Browse** to select a logo file from your computer. For best results, use a PNG file with a transparent background applied, with a maximum height of about 65 pixels. Select the image file and click on **Start Upload**. The message **Upload Complete** is displayed:

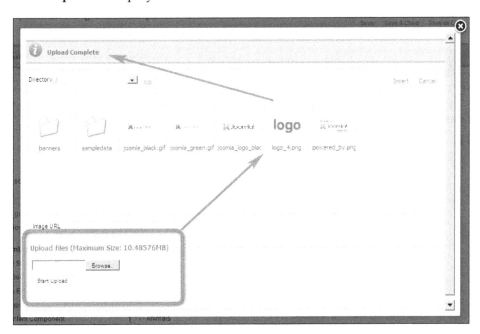

4. Click on the logo image to select it and then click on **Insert** in the top right corner.

5. In the **Edit Style** screen, click on **Save** and then click on **View Site**. The new logo image is displayed and replaces the Joomla! logo:

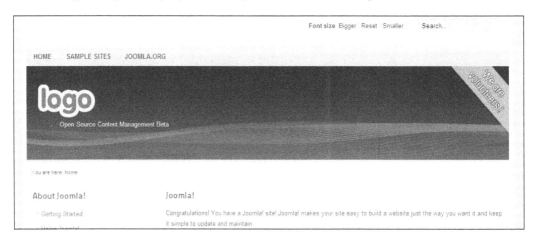

To further customize the logo and header area, enter a short description of your site in the **Advanced Options | Site Description** box. This will replace the site tag line, just below the logo.

Using a text logo

Don't have an image file to use as a logo? In the Beez 2 template, it's possible to use a text logo instead of an image. Navigate to **Template Manager | Templates** and click on the **Beez2** template name to go to the **Edit Style** page. In the **Advanced Options** panel, locate the **Logo** option and click on the **Clear** button. In the **Site Title** field, enter the text you want to be shown instead of the logo image. The site title will display as shown below:

If you're not happy with your changes, you can easily revert to the old logo image. Next to the **Logo** field, you'll find the **Select** button. Click on this to navigate to the images folder. Select **Joomla!_black.gif** and insert it.

Changing the header image file

If you use the default Beez 2 template with the **Template colour** option set to the default value (**Personal**), an image is used as the header background. This image is shown below:

Unfortunately, it's not possible to change the header image through the Template Styles options. The header image is a PNG file called `personal2.png`. It's located in a templates subfolder: `templates/beez_20/images/personal/personal2.png`.

To change the header image file, it's easiest to just replace this file by your own header graphic of choice, using FTP software. If you give the new image the same name as the existing one, you don't have to touch the CSS code referring to the graphic file. To do this, create a PNG file of 1060 x 288 pixels and call it `personal2.png`. Using FTP, upload it to the location mentioned above, replacing the existing `personal2.png` file. (You may want to first back up the original file by renaming it to something like `personal2-old.png`.)

Creating Template Styles to style individual pages

Most websites probably use just one template. Joomla! 1.6, however, allows for much more flexibility. It's possible to assign specific templates to style individual pages or groups of pages. If your site is divided into five main categories, why not use the same template in five different styles, each with their own set of options selected?

Creating and using a Template Style

Let's find out how creating and applying a Template Style works. We'll create a copy of the default Beez2 template and use it to style only the pages that are linked to through one specific menu link. In this case, we'll assign this style to the pages about Joomla! Components in the sample site:

1. Go to **Extensions | Template Manager** to access the **Template Manager: Styles** screen.

2. We'll use the Beez 2 template as the base template and create a copy of it. Select **Beez2 - Default** by ticking the select box to the left-hand side of the template name. Click on the **Duplicate** button:

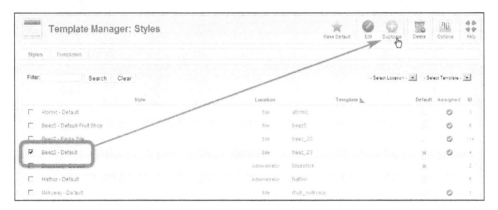

3. A copy of the template appears in the list, called **Beez2 – Default (2)**:

4. Click on the **Beez2 – Default (2)** link to edit the new style. In the **Edit Style** screen, select the settings that will distinguish this style from the default Beez 2.0 template:

a. In the **Style Name** field, enter **Beez2 – Components section**.

b. In the **Advanced Options** panel, click on the **Clear** button next to the **Logo** field. In the **Site Title** field, add **Components**. This way, the name **Components** will be displayed instead of the default graphic Joomla! logo file.

c. In the **Template colour** drop-down box, select **Nature**.

d. In the **Menus Assignment** section, tick the **Components** menu link and all the submenu items of the **Components** menu link.

The **Styles** screen should look as displayed below:

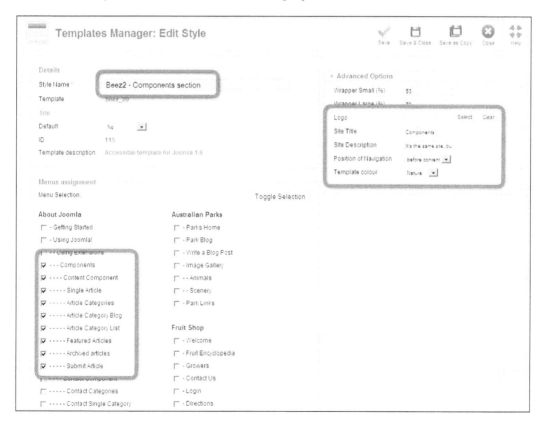

5. Click on **Save**. A message is displayed, confirming that the selected menu items have been assigned to the new template style:

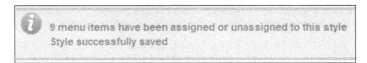

6. Click on **View Site**. On the home page and on other pages of the site, nothing has changed. In the **About Joomla!** menu, click on **Using Joomla!**, then click on **Using Extensions,** and then click on **Components**. You'll notice that the new Template Style is active:

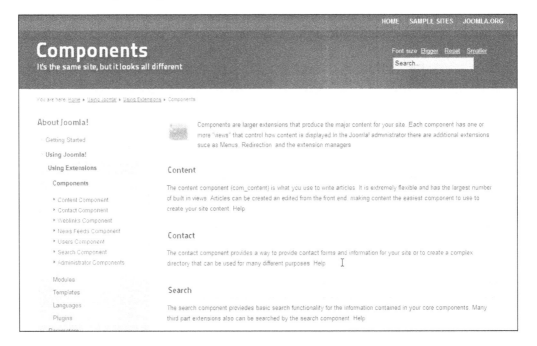

Assigning templates from the menu item itself

As templates are linked to specific menu items, wouldn't it be great if you could also assign templates (or Template Styles) directly when editing a menu link? In Joomla! 1.6, this is a welcome new feature. It means that you can control template assignment both from the template settings screen and the menu item screen. It's no longer necessary to switch to the Template Manager to control what's basically a menu item related setting.

Choosing a template from a menu item

Let's assign another page to the Template Style we just created. This time, we won't use the Template Manager, but we'll select the template from the menu link itself:

1. Go to **Menus | About Joomla**. In the **Menu Manager: Menu Items** screen, click on the link we want to edit: **Getting Started**.

2. In the **Menu Manager: Edit Menu Item** screen, you'll find the **Template Style** setting at the bottom of the **Details** section. Select the Template Style you want to apply to this page. In this example, we'll select the **Beez2 – Components section** Template Style:

3. Click on **Save & Close** and then click on **View Site**. Click on the **Getting Started** link in the **About Joomla!** menu. The selected Template Style is applied:

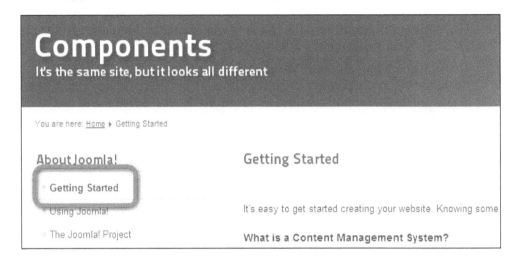

Exploring and editing installed templates

The **Template Manager | Templates** screen allows you to find out more about the templates that are installed. Here you can preview them and you can edit the template HTML and CSS files. Let's first have a look at the available templates included in the default installation of Joomla! 1.6. After that, we'll check out the ability to change the template code.

What templates are available?

Up to now, we've mainly worked with Beez 2.0, the default template in Joomla! 1.6. However, there are a few extra templates available in the Joomla! package. Navigate to **Extensions | Template Manager** and click on the **Templates** tab to go to the **Templates Manager : Templates** screen:

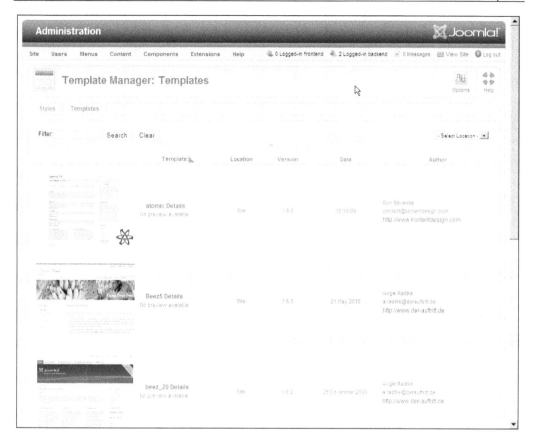

Here all available templates are displayed. In the **Location** column you can see if it's a frontend or a backend template. Joomla! comes with four frontend templates (**Location: Site**) and two templates can be used in the backend (**Location: Administrator**).

We will now look at the available templates.

atomic

New to Joomla! 1.6, **atomic** is a very basic template. It's designed as a skeleton to make your own template and to learn about Joomla! templating.

beez5

HTML5 is a new markup language for structuring and presenting content on the web. It's a major revision of the current (X)HTML standard. The **beez5** template is HTML5 ready: although by default, it uses (X)HTML code, there's a template option available to switch to HTML5 code.

beez2

This one you know: it's the new default Joomla! template. It complies with current web standards, it's flexible, and it's configurable. You've learned all about Beez 2.0 (referred to as **beez_20** in the Joomla! backend screens) in the previous sections.

bluestork

The **bluestork** template is the default template for the administrator backend. It's a complete redesign of the administrator template of 1.5. You've been introduced to bluestork in *Chapter 2* on the backend interface improvements.

hathor

The second new administrator template is called **hathor**. It's built according to accessibility rules, allowing people using different browsers and different devices to have equal access to the site. Please refer to *Chapter 2* for more information on using and adjusting this flexible and fast new backend template.

Previewing templates

To get a good impression of what any of the installed templates look like, click on the template thumbnail image in the **Templates** screen. For example, clicking on the Atomic image opens a pop-up screen displaying a bigger preview image:

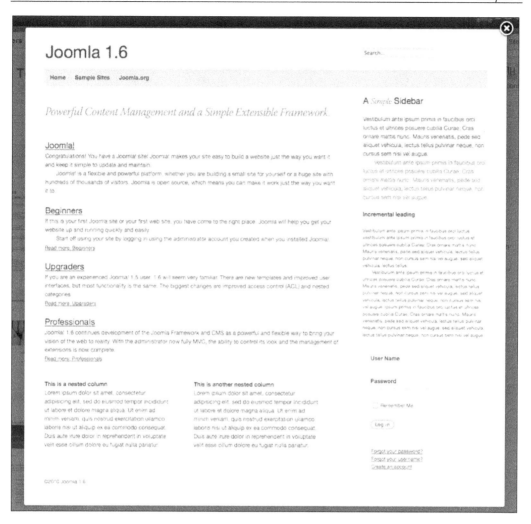

To close the preview, click on the cross in the top right-hand corner (or click anywhere in the black background area).

You've just seen a template preview—so why does the text next to the thumbnails in the **Template Manager: Templates** screen say that there's **No preview available**? That's because there are two ways to preview the available templates. As you've just seen, you can always click on the template thumbnail to see a bigger version of that image. To see a true preview, in the Template Manager **Options** the **Preview Module Positions** should be set to **Enabled**. We'll see how this works in the next section on exploring templates including their built-in module positions.

Exploring available module positions

When you activate another template, chances are, not all content will turn up in the right place (or turn up at all). This is because module positions differ from template to template: every template designer can use the module positions and module position names that fit their design best. So, when switching to a different template, it's essential to find out the available positions to be able to assign the modules in use (such as menus) to those positions. In Joomla! 1.5, you could discover module positions by adding `?tp=1` to the site url. In 1.6, there's a new method for this. Let's find out how it works:

1. Navigate to **Extensions | Template Manager** and click on the **Options** button in the toolbar:

2. In the pop-up screen, the **Templates** tab contains just one option. Set **Preview Module Positions** to **Enabled**:

3. Click on **Save & Close** to close the pop-up screen. In the **Template Manager**, click on the **Templates** tab to open the **Template Manager: Templates** screen. Since you've enabled the **Preview Module Positions** option, every template contains a preview link. Click on the **Preview** link next to the Atomic thumbnail image:

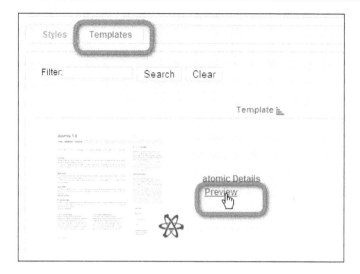

4. A preview of your site is displayed, using the Atomic template. The available module positions are shown in grey outlines; the Position name is displayed as red text:

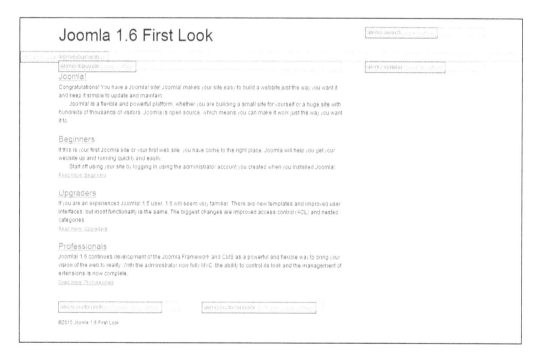

5. If you can't read the module names, it may be helpful to use your browser's zoom functionality to enlarge the current display. This way, the module position names (such as **atomic-search** and **atomic-sidebar**) are more easily readable:

If you want to use this template, you could now set it to be the default template (**Extensions | Template Manager**, select **Atomic**, click on **Make Default**) and assign the relevant modules to the appropriate positions. The technique to assign modules to positions hasn't changed since Joomla! 1.5. For example, to assign the main menu module to the **atomic-topmenu** position, open the main menu module (**Extensions | Module Manager | Main Menu**) and click on **Select Position** to assign the menu to the **atomic-topmenu** position. To see the result, click on **View Site**. Now the menu is displayed on top:

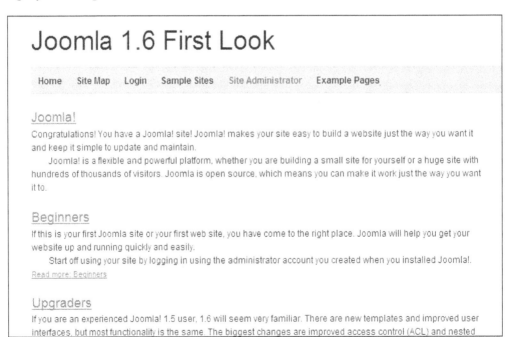

If you've followed along with the above example, you might want to go back to the default template. You'll probably know the steps involved: in the **Template Manager**, select **Beez 2 – Default** and click on **Make Default**. In the **Module Manager**, select **Main Menu** and change its position back to **position-7**.

Editing template code

Until now you've changed the design by setting the built-in template options to your taste. If you want more control over the look of your site, you can also edit the HTML and CSS code of an existing template. Joomla! 1.6 features a new editor to make this a little easier.

You can edit the code files by navigating to **Extensions | Template Manager**. Click on the **Templates** tab and then click on the **Details** link next to the template name (for example, **beez_20 Details**). Click on a filename to open the file and adjust the code. You can edit both the HTML in the main template file (index.php) and the template CSS files.

Removing the "Powered by Joomla!" text

At the bottom of the default template, the **Powered by Joomla!** text is displayed. This message is hard coded in the index.php file. To remove it, you need to remove a few lines of HTML code:

 Do be careful: if you remove too much code, the template may not function anymore.

1. In the **Template Manager**, click on the **Templates** tab. Click on the link **beez_20 Details**. You're taken to the **Customise Template** screen:

2. Click on **Edit main page template**. This opens the index.php file in an editor window. The index.php file contains the HTML source code used in the template. Now find the following code:

```
<p>
  <?php echo JText::_('TPL_BEEZ2_POWERED_BY');?>
  <a href="http://www.joomla.org/">Joomla!&#174;</a>
</p>
```

The new code editor in Joomla! 1.6 makes it a little easier to customize code, as it uses color codes to allow you to distinguish between different HTML and PHP code tags.

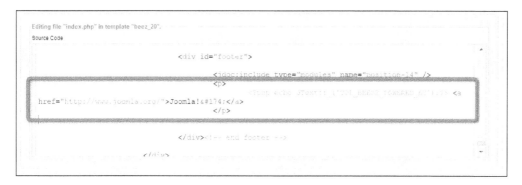

3. Select the line of copyright code and remove it. Click on **Save & Close** and then click on **View Site**. The footer text has gone.

Installing and assigning a new template

The steps involved in installing a new template haven't changed much since Joomla! 1.5. You'll download the template files as a zipped file. Go to **Extensions | Extension Manager** and upload the template ZIP file through the **Upload Package File** option.

Once it's installed, you can activate it through the **Template Styles** screen as described earlier in this chapter in the **Styles** tab: selecting templates and settings. To refresh your memory: go to **Extensions | Template Manager**, click on the **Templates** tab, select the appropriate template, and then click on **Make default**.

At the time of writing, more and more Joomla! 1.6 templates are becoming available on the web. A good example can be found at: `http://www.joomlapraise.com/blog/item/503-free-joomla-16-template`.

This is a clean and professional looking template and it's an interesting example, as it's a conversion of a Joomla! 1.5 template.

To learn more about what's needed to adapt existing templates for 1.6, have a look at: `http://www.joomlapraise.com/blog/item/520-joomla-15-to-16-template-upgrade-tutorial-part-1`.

Another useful resource on this topic is: `http://www.s-go.net/Blog/joomla-16-templates-what-designers-should-know.html`.

Finally, this is a nice instructional movie on migrating templates from 1.5 to 1.6: `http://beautyindesign.com/screencasts/tutorial-video-converting-a-joomla-1-5-template-to-1-6/`.

If you're browsing for a new template, keep in mind that templates must be suitable for Joomla! 1.6. Templates for older versions will not work.

Summary

In this chapter, we've covered the various new possibilities of using templates in Joomla! 1.6. This is what we have covered:

- Joomla! 1.6 templates now output clean code, using standards-compliant XHTML and CSS. The code is well-structured and compatible with current web standards.

- The new Template Manager interface allows you to quickly jump from the **Template Manager: Styles** tab to **Template Manager: Templates** tab.

- Template Styles are a new concept in Joomla! 1.6. You can configure any template through a series of options and save this as a Template Style. You can then assign this specific style to one or more menu items.

- It's possible to give individual pages a specific look either by assigning a Template Style to menu items from the template settings screen, or by assigning the appropriate Template Style directly from the specific menu items.

- The **Template Manager | Templates** screen allows you to explore all available templates, preview templates, and edit the template HTML and CSS files.

7
Unleashing the New Power of Extensions

Joomla! has always been famed for the fact that it's really easy to extend its basic functionality with extensions: adding new features to your website is a matter of installing an extension and changing a few settings. In Joomla! 1.6, using and maintaining extensions has become even more user-friendly and more powerful. The extensions screen has been overhauled and it contains some new functionality—such as an automated updating process for installed extensions. Moreover, there are some new modules—the very popular little functionality blocks that can appear in any position on a Joomla!-powered web page. Also, maintaining modules has become more flexible. There are new ways to control *when* (in what period of time) and *where* (on what pages) modules should appear.

In this chapter, we'll cover:

- Changes in the extensions that come with Joomla!
- The new tabbed Extension Manager screen
- Setting a time span for publishing modules
- New ways to control what pages modules are displayed on
- Finding and downloading extensions

Changes in the extensions that come with Joomla!

When you install Joomla! 1.6, it already contains a set of extensions. If you've used Joomla! 1.5, most of these will look familiar. However, there are a few changes. Let's find out which extensions have been added.

The new Redirect Manager

A new addition in 1.6 is the **Redirect Manager**, which you can find in the **Components** menu. This application can be quite useful, especially if you're migrating a 1.5 site to 1.6. When changing to a new site, many URLs from your old site are bound to change. This can result in lots of broken links from other sites that still point to the old URLs. The Redirect Manager helps you to direct visitors who come to your site through outdated links. In the **Redirect Manager**, just enter the old links and tell Joomla! what new pages it should show instead:

 To find out more about using the Redirect Manager, please have a look at *Chapter 8* on SEO changes in Joomla!

New modules to display category contents

In *Chapter 3*, you've already been introduced to two new modules allowing you to display category contents: **Articles Categories** is a simple module showing a row of hyperlinks to categories; the **Articles Category** module is more powerful and contains several options to display the actual contents of articles in a category. We'll see an example of its use later in this chapter, in the section on *New module features*.

Switching languages

Joomla! 1.6 features a basic system to create a simple, multi-language site. It allows you to create articles in different languages with their specific language set and to have these articles presented to the visitor if they choose to use this language on the site home page. To use this feature, you can install an alternative content language and enable it in the **Extensions | Language Manager** screen. In addition, you can use the **Language Switcher** module to display a list of available languages on the site, enabling visitors to switch between languages.

If your site is targeted at an international audience, you might want to try out the new content languages switching feature. Keep in mind that it is a basic system, which doesn't aim to replace dedicated multilingual content management components such as Joomfish (which allows you to manage translations, compare original texts with translations, and so on). To find out more about using different content languages using the built-in language switch, consult `http://docs.joomla.org/Language_Switcher_Tutorial_for_Joomla_1.6`. To find out more about the Joomfish extension for Joomla! 1.6, point your browser to `http://www.joomfish.net`.

No more polls

Have you recently felt the urge to take part in an online poll? Probably not! Web polls—a short question followed by a set of multiple choice answers—were a popular way to add instant interaction to websites a few years ago. Nowadays, the novelty seems to have worn off, and that's probably why the Joomla! 1.6 developers have dropped the polls component that was part of the 1.5 package. If you want to use a poll, you can use third party polls extensions for Joomla! 1.6, such as Apoll (`http://www.afactory.org`) or AcePolls (`http://www.joomace.net`).

Exploring pre-installed extensions

If you want to know more about the extensions that come with Joomla! 1.6, take some time to explore the **About Joomla! | Using Joomla! | Using Extensions** menu in the sample site data. This contains links to examples of all extensions currently on board:

To find out more about the available modules and their features, it's a good idea to explore the Module Manager. In the backend, navigate to **Extensions | Module Manager** and click on the **New** button to see a pop up screen containing a full list of available modules. If you want to know what these modules do, navigate with your mouse cursor over module names. A brief explanation appears in a pop up screen. An example is shown below:

Clicking on any of the module names takes you to the Module Manager edit screen, allowing you to browse (and set) the full set of available options for this module. If you don't want to use the module you're exploring currently, click on **Cancel** to close the screen and return to the **Module Manager: Modules** overview.

The new Extension Manager screen

Compared to previous versions of Joomla!, the **Extension Manager** is finally worth its name: the new options here give you new control over extensions. Navigate to **Extensions | Extension Manager** (the comparable menu option was previously called **Extensions | Install/Uninstall**) to have a look at the new layout and functionality:

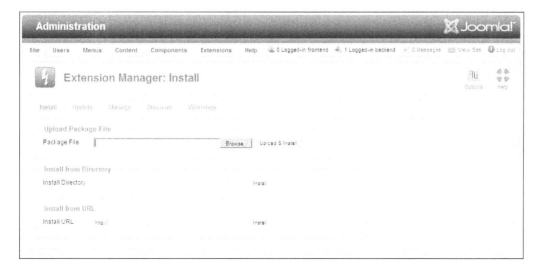

In Joomla! 1.5, the main purpose of the Extension Manager screen was to allow you to install or uninstall extensions. Although you'll still see the familiar **Extension Manager: Install** functionality when you open this screen in Joomla! 1.6, you'll notice that the Extension Manager now contains four additional tabs, apart from the default **Install** view: **Update**, **Manage**, **Discover**, and **Warnings**.

Tab 1: Install

The **Install** screen allows you to install any type of extension: components, modules, plugins, language packs, and templates. As before, three installation methods are available, but most users will only need the most common one, **Upload Package File**. Here you can upload a downloaded extension file (usually a ZIP file) and install it in one click using the **Upload & Install** button.

Tab 2: Update

There can be a disadvantage to using extensions: it can mean that a substantial amount of the functionality of your site relies not on Joomla! itself, but on add-ons created by numerous other developers. How do you keep track of the updates those developers create for all the extensions you're deploying? Even if you have just one site with a dozen extensions, checking for updates regularly takes a lot of time. You have to keep an eye on the Joomla! Extensions Database (`http://extensions.Joomla.org`) or the developers' sites to see if there are updates. You can imagine how much effort it would take to run even more extension-rich sites. In real life, this means that many Joomla! site owners are running outdated extensions, which can cause all kinds of problems (especially regarding site security).

This is where Joomla! 1.6's new Extension Manager Update functionality comes to the rescue. It makes keeping your site up-to-date effortless:

The **Update** screen allows you to update installed extensions. With one click, you can search for updates for all installed extensions. If an extension supports this feature, you can update it without having to first find the update on the Web, download it, and install the update through the **Install** screen.

After you've clicked the **Update** button, you'll see a notice telling you whether updates are available. If they are, you can automatically install them using the **Update** button. The updating process is fully automated. After completion, a message is displayed that the available updates have been installed successfully.

> In principle, you can now find updates for all installed extensions with just one click. However, the **Update** functionality only works for extensions that support it. It's to be expected that this feature will be widely supported by extension developers, but for other extensions you'll still have to manually check for updates by visiting the extension developer's website.

Tab 3: Manage

The **Manage** screen provides you with an overview of all the installed extensions. You can use the **Enable** button to enable (or publish) selected extensions. The **Disable** button is used to unpublish extensions. To remove extensions that you don't use any more, select the extension and click on the **Uninstall** button in the toolbar:

Tab 4: Discover

In exceptional cases, extensions can't be installed the normal way, using the **Install** button. This can occur when the installation files are too large, which some web server configurations don't allow. You can still install these extensions by directly uploading the files to the appropriate folders on your web server through FTP. After that, click on the **Discover** button to detect the extension and then click on the **Install** button to install it through this alternative method:

Tab 5: Warnings

If the extensions you use work properly, the **Warnings** screen should display a **No warnings detected** message. If there are any technical issues concerning the (combination of) extensions you have installed, the screen contains warnings:

New module features

In Joomla! 1.6, using modules is more flexible:

- You can schedule the time during which a module should display. In previous versions of Joomla!, you could set a start date and an end date for publishing articles. Now this is also possible for modules.

- Modules are always assigned to one or more menu items. However, when editing a menu in Joomla! 1.5, there was no way to find out or change which modules were assigned to that menu item. You had to leave the menu item edit screen, navigate to the particular module's settings in the Module

Manager, and check the module's menu assignment there. In Joomla! 1.6, you can set what modules are assigned to a menu link directly when you're editing a menu link.

Let's find out how you can put these two new features to use in your day-to-day web building practice. First, we'll try out how to set timed modules, and after that, we'll look at the different ways to assign modules to menu items.

Setting a time span for publishing modules

Being able to schedule module display is great if—for example—you want to have a banner promoting a temporary action and set it to be published automatically until the last day of the action. Another use of this new feature is to temporarily draw some extra attention to a particular section of the site. We'll experiment with this using the Joomla! sample site.

Creating a scheduled module

Let's assume that you've found that your site visitors tend to overlook a particular site section—for example, the blog pages on your site. Why don't you put a temporary little block with teaser contents on the site to promote the blog? This would give you the opportunity to find out what the effects of such a module are on the number of visitors that actually click on the teaser links to visit the site blog.

For this, you can use the new **Articles Category** module. Let's create this module and schedule the publication date:

1. Go to **Extensions | Module Manager**. Click on the **New** button.

2. A pop up screen with module names appears. In this list, click on **Articles Category**:

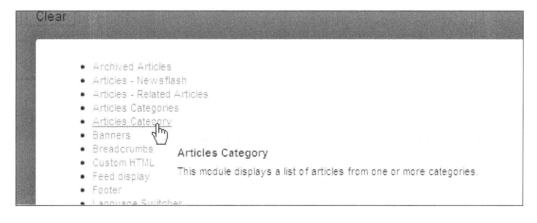

3. In the **Module Articles Category** screen, enter the desired values and settings:

   ° In the **Title** field, enter **This Month's Spotlight**.

   ° In the **Show Title** section, select **Show**.

   ° Click on the **Select** button next to the **Position** field. In the pop up box, select **position-6**.

4. Now let's make the module appear for just one month. Click on the calendar icon next to **Start Publishing** and select today's date in the calendar pop up. The pop up will then close:

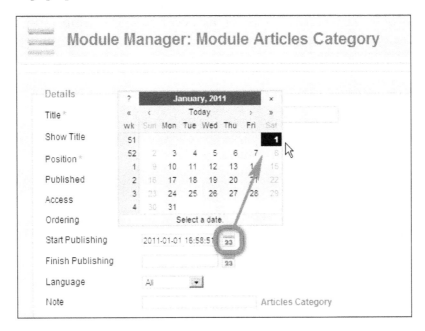

5. Click on the calendar icon next to **Finish Publishing** and select a future date in the calendar pop up. The pop up will then close.

6. In the **Filtering Options** panel on the right-hand side of the screen, select the **Park Blog** category:

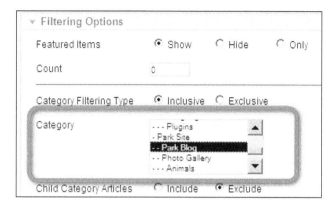

In this way, articles from this category will appear in the **Articles Category** listing.

7. In the **Display Options** panel, set **Introtext** to **Show**. In this way, the module will display the first few lines of the text of the article. By default, this is restricted to the first 100 characters, but you can enter any other value in the **Introtext Limit** field:

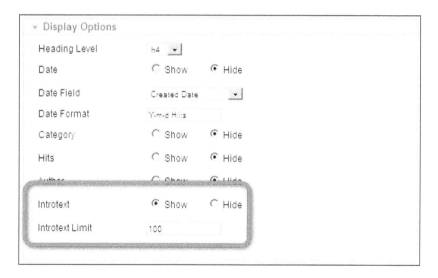

8. Click on **Save & Close** and then click on **View Site** to see the output on the frontend. The module is displayed in a new column on the right-hand side:

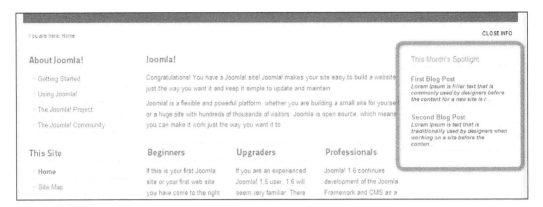

 If the module doesn't appear on the frontend, check the date settings. If the **Start Publishing** date is set in the future, the module won't be displayed now. Also, make sure that you've set your time zone correctly in the configuration. See **Site | Global Configuration | Server | Location Settings | Server Time Zone**.

Now you've created a great little teaser block, drawing attention to the articles in the blog section. You could also use the scheduled modules feature to create a set of modules, each published for one month. This way, you can schedule a set of consecutive teaser modules, each drawing attention to a part of your site for a specific period.

Making use of the new Note field

The module edit screen in Joomla! 1.6 contains a new field, called **Note**. Here you can add a short note for yourself or your fellow web team members. For example, you can put a little reminder here about the nature of this module. If you enter "only displayed for one month", you'll easily remember why and how you've deployed this particular module when you stumble upon it a few months later:

The **Note** text is visible in the module edit screen, but you'll notice that notes are also displayed in the **Module Manager: Modules** overview screen, just below the module name. All in all, this small addition provides you with a nifty little system to add short messages for anyone browsing the modules listing:

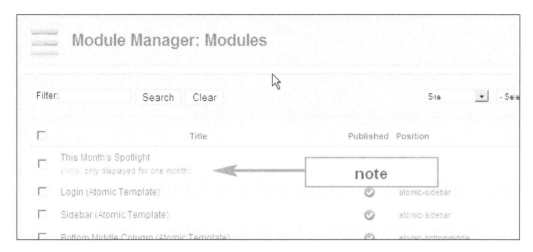

Assigning a module to specific menu items

Previously, assigning a module to specific menu items could be quite a bit of work. To refresh your memory, here's what the Menu Assignment feature looked like in the old days of Joomla! 1.5:

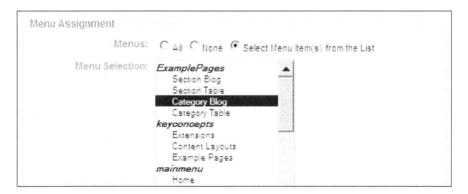

If you had to select many items on a site with lots of menu links, this would involve some serious clicking while holding the *Shift* or *Ctrl* key. Moreover, it was very easy to accidentally undo the selection you'd just made—which meant that you'd have to start selecting things all over again.

In Joomla! 1.6, selecting menu items is much more user-friendly. Menus are presented within tabbed panels, and selecting menu items is done by ticking the checkboxes next to the menu items. Moreover, you can now choose to publish through the **On all pages except those selected** setting, and you can use the **Toggle Selection** button "invert" all current selections in all menus:

Assigning a module to all pages except a few

In the previous exercise, you created an **Articles Category** module using just the default **Menu Assignment** settings. By default, a new module is assigned to all pages (that is, all menu links). Let's change this and publish the module on all pages, except for the actual blog pages this module links to:

1. Go to **Extensions | Module Manager** and locate the module that you created earlier in this chapter: **This Month's Spotlight**. Click on the module title to edit the module settings. (Of course, you can select any other module to try this out.)

2. In the **Menu Assignment** panel at the bottom-left of the window, select **On all pages except those selected**. All menu items remain selected.

3. Click on the **Toggle Selection** button to deselect all items.

4. To make the module not appear on the blog pages, first click on the **Australian Parks** tab, and then select **Park Blog** in the menu list:

5. Click on **Save & Close**.

That's all there is to it! The module is now still displayed on all the pages. However, when you browse the pages displayed through the **Park Blog** menu link, the module isn't shown any more:

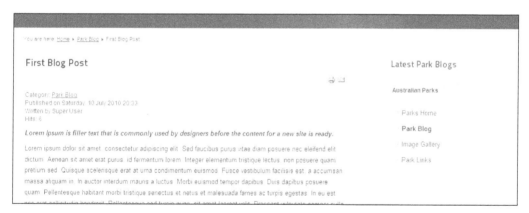

Assigning modules from the menu item settings

You've just selected the pages that you wanted a module to appear on, by editing the module settings. In Joomla! 1.5, this was the only way to assign modules to a menu item. In Joomla! 1.6, there is an additional and more logical way to control on which pages modules appear: you can set module assignment from any menu item itself (via the **Edit Menu Item** screen).

To access the **Edit Menu Item** screen, go to **Menus | Menu Manager | Menus** and select the menu that you want to inspect. Click on the name of any menu link to open the **Edit Menu Item** screen. This now contains a new panel, called **Module Assignment for this Menu Item** on the right-hand side of the window:

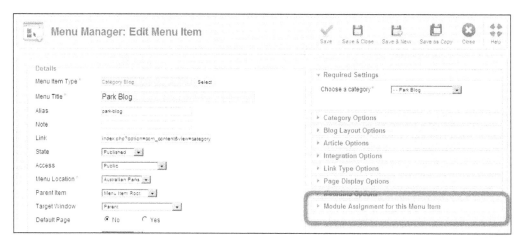

Click on the panel title to see a list of *all* available modules — not just those assigned to this particular menu item. This way, you can control where modules appear (and change other settings) from the menu link itself.

Changing module settings via the Edit Menu Item screen

Earlier, we set a module not to appear on the Park Blog pages of the sample site. Now let's assume we want to change this. Of course, you could locate the desired module through the Module Manager and change its settings, but you can now alternatively go to the **Park Blog** menu item itself and use the **Module Assignment for this Menu Item** panel to set the modules settings. Let's find out how the latter option works:

1. Navigate to **Menus | Australian Parks** and click on the **Park Blog** menu link to edit it:

2. The **Menu Manager: Edit Menu Item** opens. In the right-hand column, click on the heading of the **Module Assignment for this Menu Item** panel:

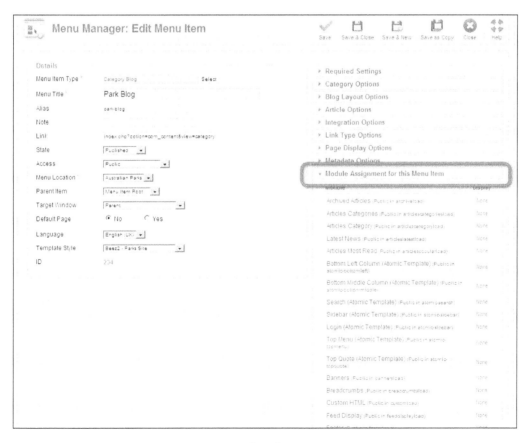

3.   Click on the module title **This Month's Spotlight**:

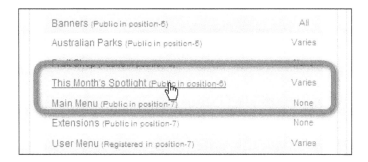

4.   Now the module details—including the **Menu Assignment** settings—are shown in a pop up screen:

5.   In the **Menu Assignment** section, you can see the menu items the module is assigned to. These are the exact same settings you've selected earlier on, through the Module Manager:

6. To make the module display on all pages, change the value **Module Assignment** in the drop-down box to **On all pages**. Click on **Save & Close** to close the pop up screen and return to the **Edit Menu Item** screen.

7. Click on **Save** and then click on **View Site** to see the output on the frontend. The module is now displayed on all the site pages, including the Blog pages.

In *Chapter 4* about menus, we've already had a look at the Module Assignment for this Menu Item box. Please refer to that chapter to find out more about how to change module assignment directly from the module edit screen.

Displaying available module positions

When using modules, it's important to know which module positions are available in the current template. In *Chapter 6*, you've already seen how to get a visual overview of the module positions that are built into the template. In short: navigate to **Extensions | Template Manager** and click on the **Options** button in the toolbar. Make sure that **Preview Module Positions** is set to **Enabled**. Now you can preview the available positions in the **Template Manager**: click on the **Templates** tab and then click on the **Preview** link next to the template thumbnail image. This will display a preview of the site using the selected template. The preview displays red outlines indicating the available module positions and their position names.

Finding and downloading extensions for Joomla! 1.6

The process of downloading and installing extensions hasn't changed in version 1.6. The Joomla! Extensions Directory (`http://extensions.Joomla.org`) offers a great overview of the extensions currently available. At the time of writing, more and more extensions are becoming available for Joomla! 1.6. To make sure that the extension you want to download and install is ready for Joomla! 1.6, check for the **1.6 Native** label in the **Compatibility** information for the extension:

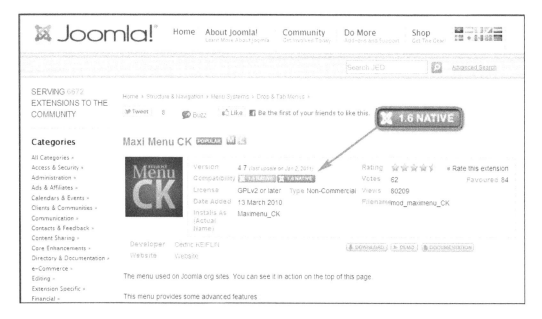

To see a list of all extensions that are compatible with Joomla! 1.6, in the Joomla Extensions Directory, click on **Advanced Search** and select **1.6 Native** in the **Compatibility** drop-down box.

> If you're interested in developing extensions for Joomla! yourself, consult http://www.joomla.org/16/features/developer.html. This page contains an overview of technical changes in the software that are relevant to developers and also provides links to several resources about developing for Joomla! 1.6. You can also find some great developer resources and links to tutorial videos at http://brian.teeman.net/joomla-1.6/everything-you-wanted-to-know-about-joomla-16-but-were-afraid-to-ask.html.

Summary

In this chapter, we've covered what's new in using extensions for Joomla! 1.6:

- The collection of extensions that comes with Joomla! 1.6 shows some welcome new additions. A new component is Redirect Manager, used to redirect visitors from outdated URLs to new URLs.

- New modules include Article Categories and Articles Category, used to present categories and their contents.

- The new Extension Manager screen contains five tabs, each featuring its own specific functionality: Install, Update, Manage, Discover, and Warnings.

- The new Extension Manager Update functionality simplifies the process of updating installed extensions.

- In Joomla! 1.6, you can schedule the time during which a module should be displayed.

- Assigning modules to menu items has become much easier. For example, you can now choose to display a module on all pages, except the ones selected. Moreover, you can now select module assignment directly from the Edit Menu Item screen.

8
SEO Improvements

There are a number of things you can do to make it easier for search engines to find and index your content and improve your chances of being well ranked in the search results lists. Luckily, Joomla! 1.6 offers some important new features for Search Engine Optimization (SEO).

In this chapter, you'll learn more about:

- The SEO advantages of the new semantic HTML output
- Configuring metadata and HTML page titles
- Using search engine friendly URLs
- Helping search engines to find all content: using a site map
- Restoring broken links: redirecting search engines to new URLs

The SEO bonus of well structured layouts

In *Chapter 6* on templates, you've seen that Joomla! now outputs clean code, using semantic HTML layouts. Joomla! 1.5 wasn't up to web standards in this respect. For one thing, it used tables to create page layouts, which is generally regarded nowadays as one of the biggest no-no's in semantic coding terms. Another drawback of the 1.5 output was that HTML heading elements, such as H1 and H2, weren't used as they should has been (notably, to properly structure the HTML document).

In Joomla! 1.6, HTML elements are used with respect to their intended purpose within the document. Tables aren't used for layout purposes anymore; headings now define the main structure of the HTML document. This is great, as it will make it easier for search engines to unravel the structure of the web page and to find out what content is relevant and worth indexing.

The new semantic HTML layouts are a big step forward towards a SEO friendly site — and the great news is that you don't have to do anything to achieve it, as it's now all part of the default Joomla! output. We will, however, have a quick look at the use of heading elements, as you'll partly apply those yourself when creating or editing articles.

 If you want to read more on web standards and semantic code, please refer to *Chapter 6* on the new table-less templates in Joomla! 1.6.

Proper use of HTML heading elements

The screenshot below gives you an impression of the default heading formatting in Joomla! 1.6:

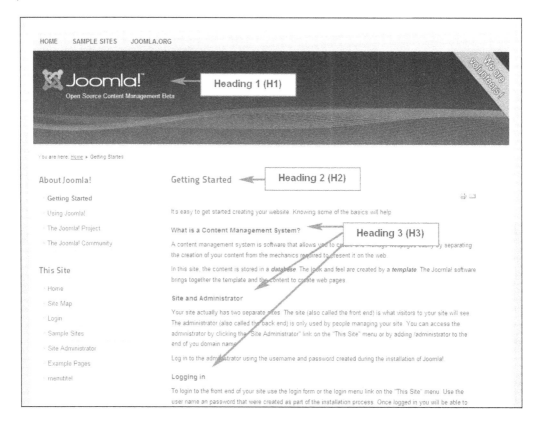

Joomla! now uses H1 for the site name or logo. The second heading level, H2, is used for the main content headings. On an article page such as the one shown in the screenshot above, H2 is the article title. In previous versions of Joomla!,

page headings would be styled using proprietary CSS style names such as
`.contentheading`, which were of little use to search engines. Although there's
some debate as to the proper use of `H1` headings and the Joomla! 1.6 solution isn't the
definite answer (See *What's the best way to use the H1 element?* section below), this new
default usage of headings is certainly a huge improvement in terms of SEO-friendly
page markup.

Building on the new basic HTML output, you can now easily create pages that follow
this structure:

- `H1`: site title/logo
- `H2`: article heading
- `H3` – `H6`: article subheadings

Adding H3 through H6 headings

Make sure to keep to the hierarchical heading structure when writing and editing
articles yourself. For example, don't just used bold text to create a heading for a page
section, but apply the appropriate headings in the Joomla! article editor.

The article editor **Format** drop-down box allows you to apply any heading tag from
`H1` to `H6`. As `H1` is already used for the site title and `H2` is used for the article title, you
should use only `H3`, `H4`, `H5`, and `H6` headings within an article's text:

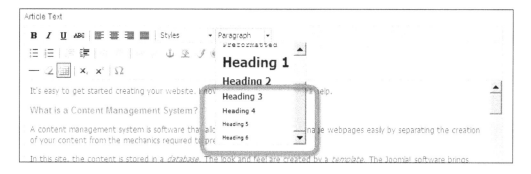

Adding an alternative H1 page heading

You've seen that Joomla! 1.6 uses the HTML `H1` element for the site title. However,
the site title gives generic information about the site, not about the current page.
That's why you might choose to add an alternative (second) `H1` element, acting as a
separate top-level heading that specifies the content of the current page.

This way, you can have a page structure like this:

- H1: site title (for example, ACME Web Design Blog)
- H1: main page heading (for example, Web Design Trends)
- H2: article heading (for example, An Overview of Current Web Layouts)
- H3 – H6: article subheadings

What's the best way to use the H1 element?

There is some discussion as to how the H1 element should be applied within a HTML page structure. Some argue the H1 element should only be used for the main page heading. If a H1 is used for the site name or logo (which is the Joomla! 1.6 practice), all pages in the site share the same H1 information. Wouldn't it be better to use H1 strictly for the main heading, containing meaningful information on the specific contents of the page?

There's no clear-cut answer to this question; there's even a website dedicated to this one dilemma ... (http://www.h1debate.com). To be on the safe side, you may want to choose to use two H1s for both the logo and the main page heading. In Joomla! 1.6, this is now possible. And according to Google specialists, using multiple H1s on any page is allowed. As Google puts it: use H1 where it makes sense; use it sparingly, but it's okay to use it multiple times on a page. (See Google's video called *More than one H1 on a page: good or bad?* on YouTube at http://www.youtube.com/watch?v=GIn5qJKU8VM&NR=1)

In Joomla! 1.6, adding an alternative H1 page heading is possible for any menu link item type: whatever menu link you create, in the **New Menu Item** screen, you'll find the option to add a specific **Page Heading** under the **Page Display Options**. This means that you can specify the H1 heading for any article that's directly linked to through a menu item.

Let's find out how you can add a specific H1 page title to an article. To see how this works, we'll edit the menu link pointing to the Getting Started article in the sample data:

1. In the backend, go to **Menus | About Joomla!** to display the menu items. Click on the top link in the list, **Getting started**, to edit this menu item. The **Menu Manager: Edit Menu Item** screen opens.

2. Click on the **Page Display Options** panel name on the right-hand side of the screen to open this panel.

3. Set **Show Page Heading** to **Yes** to make sure that the new **Page Heading** will be displayed on the page.

4. In the **Page Heading** field enter a heading text. As we just want to test things out, you can enter something like **A H1 Page Heading**. (If you don't enter anything here, the Page Heading will just repeat the Menu Link text. This isn't what you want, as Joomla! already displays the menu link text as a H2 element above the article—so you'd end up with both an H1 and an H2 heading sharing the same text):

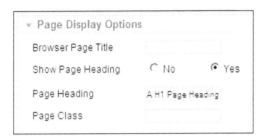

5. Click on **Save & Close** and then click on **View Site**. On the frontend, click on the **Getting started** link in the **About Joomla!** menu to see what's changed.

You'll notice that the new Page Heading (a Heading 1 element) is displayed just above the page title (a Heading 2 element):

Page Heading and Page Title – what's the difference?

You may be confused by the **Page Display Options** panel: apart from the **Page Heading** field, there also is a field called **Browser Page Title**. The Browser Page Title is the text contained in the HTML `title` element, whereas the Page Heading is the text in the H1 element. In other words, Joomla! now allows you to set both the `title` element and the H1 element for any menu item just as you like. You'll learn more about changing the HTML page title (or **Browser Page Title**, as Joomla! calls it) in the next section.

Configuring HTML page titles

It's considered good SEO practice to not only add a specific page heading (contained in the H1 element), but to also make sure that each page has a descriptive HTML page title (the title element). Page titles are one of the most important ranking factors for search engines, so it's important to make sure they contain relevant information about the content.

The contents of the title element aren't displayed on the web page itself, but they're shown in the browser title bar. The screenshot below shows how the page title **Using Joomla!** is displayed in Mozilla Firefox:

In most browsers, the page title is also displayed in the current browser tab, as shown in the screenshot below (taken from Google Chrome):

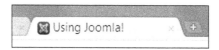

Setting the HTML page title

By default, Joomla! bases the HTML page title upon the menu link text (the menu item Title). However, you can also control the page title text manually. If you want the HTML page title to be different from the menu item title, you can set a specific HTML page title in the Menu Link details. Let's find out how this works:

1. Navigate to **Menus | Menu Manager** and select the menu containing the link you want to edit. In this example, let's select the **About Joomla!** menu.

2. Click on the **Using Joomla!** link to edit it. In the **Page Display Options** panel, enter the desired **Browser Page Title** text. For the purposes of this example, you can enter something like **Browser Page Title set in Menu Item**:

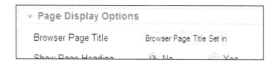

3 Click on **Save & Close** and then click on **View Site** to see the output on the frontend. Navigate to the menu item that you've changed to see the new title in the browser title bar (and in the current browser tab):

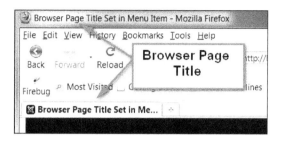

 You've just seen how to control the Browser Page Title by editing the Menu Item details. However, you can't change the Page Title for an article that isn't directly linked to through a menu link. If, for example, an article is displayed through a link on a Category Blog page, Joomla! will base the Browser Page Title on the article Title (set in the article edit screen details).

Adding the Site Name to the page title

Another way to configure the HTML page title is to append the Site Name to it. This is the name that you've entered when installing Joomla! and that you can also enter or change in the **Site Name** field found through **Site | Global Configuration | Site Settings**.

In Joomla! 1.5, it wasn't possible to include the site name in the HTML page title. The page title shown in the browser title bar was only based upon the current article heading or page heading. The benefit of having the option to add the site name is that all the pages will display both information about the site *and* about the current page contents. If your organization feels that having its brand in the title is important, now you can add it through a site-wide option in the **Global Configuration** settings.

To try this out, navigate to **Site | Global Configuration**. In the **SEO settings** section, a new option is available: **Include Site Name in Page Titles**. If this option is set to **No** (which is the default value), the page title will be taken from the current article heading or page heading. For example, the page title for the Getting Started page in the sample data is **Getting Started**, as shown in the screenshot below:

If you choose **Yes** in the **Include Site Name in Page Titles** option, the site name will be added. For example, if you have entered **Your Site Name** as the site name, the page title will change as follows:

In this example, the text **Your Site Name** is added to the HTML page title.

Try and keep the full HTML title short; preferably it shouldn't be more than 64 characters. In browser window titles, browser tabs, and in search engine listings, there is only limited room.

Should you always choose to put the brand name or site name before the page topic in the HTML title? For search engines, the first word in the title tag is most relevant. When you expect people to search for your brand name, putting it in the HTML title can boost your ranking. But if people search specifically for the topics of your pages — and your site name or brand name isn't well known or doesn't describe the topic — you might want to leave the option to add the site name to all page titles unchecked.

Entering site metadata

If you have some experience building websites, you're probably familiar with adding metadata information to pages. Metadata are added to the HTML document source code. It's information that's not displayed on the web page, but search engine spiders do process it. Search engines may present the content of the meta description tag in the search results page. Although meta keywords aren't of vital importance for major search engines anymore, it certainly won't hurt to add meaningful metadata to your site. In Joomla! 1.6, you have a little more control over the metadata that will be used in your site pages.

In Joomla! 1.5, the global site metadata were filled by default with some standard text about Joomla! itself. This didn't work out well: many site administrators didn't bother to change the default text, which meant that their sites were indexed by search engines using the wrong information. Instead of describing what the site was about, the metadata contained useless information about the CMS used to construct the site.

In Joomla! 1.6, the site-wide metadata fields are empty, so even if you don't change anything, your site won't be indexed using information about the Joomla! CMS. Moreover, you can now enter the appropriate global metadata right from the very start. When installing Joomla!, you'll notice that the **Configuration** screen (step 6 of the Joomla! installer) contains a new section, called **Advanced Settings – Optional**. Click on this heading to enter the **Meta Description** for your site and the **Meta Keywords**, as shown below:

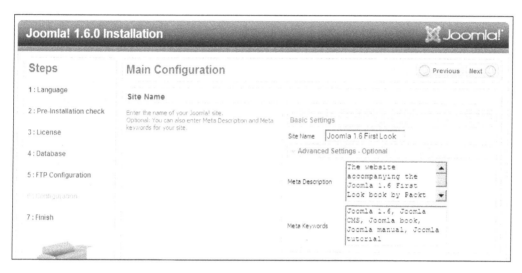

If you want to skip this step and go on installing Joomla! first, you can still enter metadata later. To do this, in the backend of the site, navigate to **Site | Global Configuration**. In the **Site** screen, the metadata can be entered or edited in the **Metadata Settings** section:

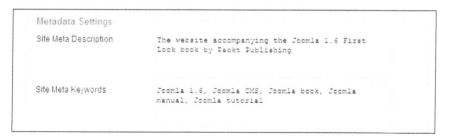

 It's a good idea to keep your meta description as concise as possible. Google will only use the first 155 characters.

Entering metadata for menu items, categories, and articles

Site-wide metadata information is useful, but it's even better to add specific metadata for other content. In Joomla! 1.6, you can enter metadata on four levels:

- Site-wide, through Global Configuration (already possible in 1.5)
- For individual menu links (new in 1.6)
- For individual *categories* (new in 1.6)
- For individual articles (already possible in 1.5)

This means that you can override the global metadata description and keywords on three sublevels. Which of these meta tags are used on the actual web page? The principle is that metadata set on more specific levels override other metadata. In other words:

1. Global metadata are used if you haven't set other meta information.

2. You can override the global data by entering metadata for specific menu items. As you can see in the screenshot below, entering these metadata is done in the **Metadata Options** panel in the **Edit Menu Item** (or **New Menu Item**) screen:

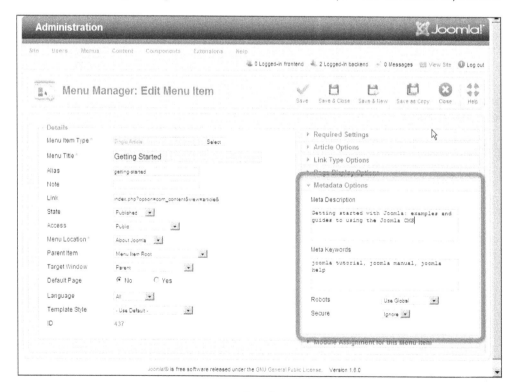

3. Metadata for a category override global metadata or menu item metadata. New in version 1.6, you can add a meta description and keywords for categories. This isn't just possible for articles categories. You can also enter metadata for categories in other components, such as Banners categories or Contacts categories. In the screenshot below, the **Metadata Options** panel for the **Edit an Articles Category** screen is shown. Again, the screen layout and options are comparable to the metadata sections in other parts of the Joomla! backend:

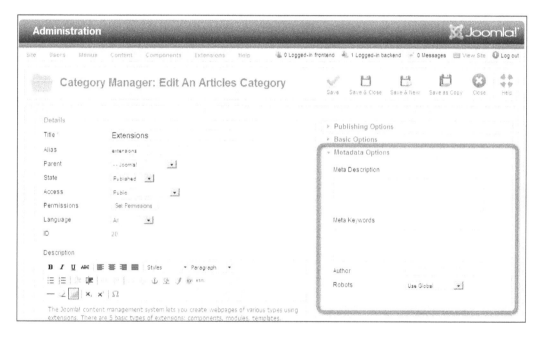

4. Finally, you can set metadata on the level of individual articles. These override global, menu item, or category metadata. Again, you'll find the metadata options in the **Metadata Options** panel, as shown in the screenshot below:

Choosing what metadata to set

Now that you can set metadata on four levels, do you need to use them all? It's always a good idea to set global metadata, as this provides search engines with general information on the nature of your site. You can choose to set metadata for specific menu items, categories, and individual pages if these menu items, categories, or pages are important from a SEO point of view. But there will probably be many pages that you don't have to bother adding metadata for; for example, a Site Policy page or a Disclaimer article are probably much less important than specific pages describing the services or products you want to sell.

Using search engine friendly URLs

Although the SEO settings of Joomla! 1.6 have remained unchanged, there's still a big improvement: by default, Search Engine Friendly URLs are now turned on. In **SEO Settings** (found via the **Site | Global Configuration | Site** tab) the **Search Engine Friendly URLs** option is set to **Yes**:

This means that Joomla! sites no longer output unreadable URLs like the ones common to the previous version:

`http://www.example.com/index.php?option=com_content&view=article&id=8.`

The new default Joomla! 1.6 URLs are much shorter and easier to understand:

`http://www.example.com/index.php/getting-started.`

This is good news for site administrators, as they don't have to change any settings here. The default URLs are fine for search engines.

> There's still some room for improvement: all default Joomla! URLs still share the `index.php` bit. You can get rid of this part of the URLs by using the **Use Apache mod_rewrite** option, found in the **SEO settings** section. However, this requires a bit more work than just setting this option to **Yes**. If your site is hosted on an Apache-powered web server (which is very common), you'll also have to rename the `htaccess.txt` file in the Joomla! root folder on the web server to `.htaccess` (with a leading dot). Not all hosting providers allow you to use `.htaccess` files or have the necessary Apache module installed. If you're not sure whether your account supports this, check with your hosting provider.

Adding a site map

In *Chapter 3*, you were introduced to the new nested category system in Joomla! Nested categories don't just give you more flexibility in structuring your site content, but they also have SEO advantages. By creating a logical, systematic structure for all articles, you'll enable both human visitors and search engines to quickly find their way.

Moreover, you can now easily create a simple site map: a list of links to all categories on the site. Adding a site map is also regarded as good SEO practice, as it enables search engine spiders to detect what your site has to offer.

Joomla! 1.6 enables you to add a site map, using a new menu item type called **List All Categories**. We've covered this in *Chapter 3*. If you want to see how the site map in the Joomla! default sample data is set up, have a look at the *New category view # 1: List All Categories* section in *Chapter 3*. If you want to create a basic site map for yourself using the List All Categories menu item type, see *Creating a link to a site map* in *Chapter 3*.

Using the Xmap site map extension

Joomla!'s built-in site map functionality is not a replacement for specific site map extensions. Such extensions contain more options to show all the available content on the site (not just articles) and they automatically generate XML files for search engines. Using an XML site map is the preferred way to present site map information for search engines. A great (and free) site map extension for Joomla! 1.6 is Xmap.

To get an idea of the extra features as compared to the standard Joomla! site map capabilities, let's try out this extension:

1. Go to http://extensions.joomla.org/extensions/structure-a-navigation/site-map/3066. Click on **Download** to go to the developer's website. On this site, click on the **Download** link for the Xmap release for Joomla! 1.6 (at the time of writing, this is Xmap 2.0 Beta 2 for Joomla 1.6).

2. Save the extension ZIP file to your computer. To install the extension, navigate to **Extensions | Extension Manager**. In the **Upload Package File** section, click on the **Browse** button to select the downloaded zip file. Click on **Upload & Install** to install the extension. A message will appear indicating you've successfully installed Xmap.

3. Go to **Components | Xmap**. In the toolbar, click on **New** to create a site map. The **New Sitemap** screen is displayed:

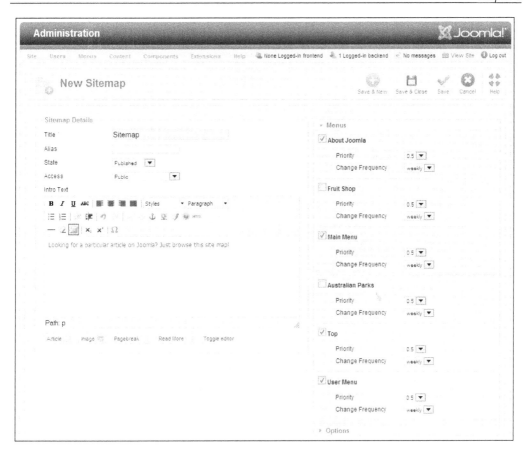

4. In the **Sitemap Details** section, enter a **Title** (such as Sitemap) and enter a
    short **Intro Text** that will be displayed on the site map page. Change the
    State to **Published**. In the **Menus** panel on the right-hand side of the screen,
    select the menus which contain the contents that you want to add to the
    site map.

5. To change the order of the menus and get the Main Menu contents to display
    at the top of the site map list, in the **Menus** panel, click on the **Main Menu**
    panel and drag the panel to the top of the list. Click on **Save & Close**.

6. To create a menu link pointing to the site map, go to **Menus | Main Menu**
    and click on the **New** button. Click on the **Select** button next to the **Menu
    Item Type** field. In the menu item type pop-up window, there's a new
    section called **Xmap**. Select **HTML Site Map**. The pop-up window closes.

7. In the **Required Settings** section, click on **Change** to select the site map that
    you've just created.

8. Enter some text as the **Menu Title** that will appear in the menu. Leave the other settings unchanged and click on **Save & Close**.

9. It would be confusing to have two site map links on your site, so let's unpublish the **Site Map** link that's already part of the Joomla! sample data. Go to **Menus | Main Menu**. Select the **Site Map** link and click on the **Unpublish** button.

10. On the frontend of your site, click on the new **Site Map** link at the bottom of the Main Menu. The site map is displayed. As you can see, it's a more detailed site map than the one that you can create using the List All Categories menu item type. The Xmap sitemap contains links to all the content that's linked to through the selected menus on the site:

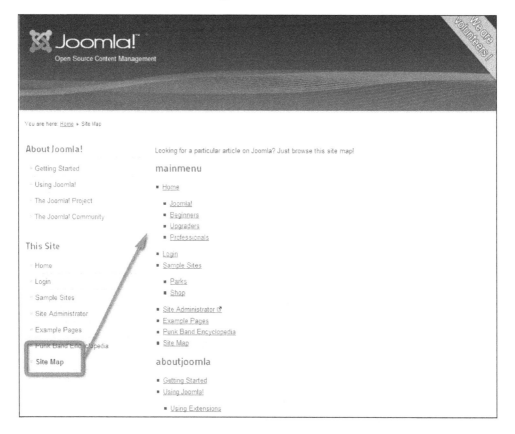

Xmap is a powerful extension. It allows you to create XML site map files for search engine robots and to make more than one site map with different preferences for each sitemap. To find out more about the possibilities of Xmap, consult http://joomla.vargas.co.cr/en/documentation/27-xmap.

Using the new Redirect Manager

In the **Components** menu, you may have noticed a new addition in 1.6: the **Redirect Manager**. It works in conjunction with a plugin called **Redirect**, which is also part of the default installation and which is enabled by default. The Redirect Manager and plugin keep track of any "page not found" errors that occur when visitors are trying to visit pages in the current domain that have been removed or deleted. In the Redirect Manager screen, these URL errors are listed. This way, you can keep an eye on the old URLs that still attract visitors, but just generate "page not found" errors. For each of these URLs, you can choose to redirect future visitors to the right pages.

This feature can be quite useful, especially if you're migrating a Joomla! 1.5 site to 1.6. URLs from your old site are bound to change, resulting in broken links from other sites that still point to expired URLs. The Redirect Manager helps you to direct visitors from expired URLs to new URLs).

Using URL redirection will also help search engine spiders to detect valuable content, instead of just hitting a dead-end error page. This helps you to preserve the search engine page ranking after the URLs of existing pages on your site have changed.

> There are other ways to create page redirects, using .htaccess files. These require some more effort: you'll have to manually create lists of old and new URLs and put or edit a special .htaccess file on your web server. For more information, see http://www.tamingthebeast. net/articles3/spiders-301-redirect.htm.

Creating page redirects

Let's assume you've replaced your old site with a brand new one, built with Joomla! 1.6. You'd probably make a list of relevant old URLs (the key pages of your old site) and the new URLs (the pages you want to redirect your visitors to).

In this exercise, we'll look at how the Redirect Manager component works by entering a non-existent old URL and telling the Redirect Manager what new page it should show instead:

1. Go to **Components | Redirect** to open the **Redirect Manager: Links** screen:

You'll recognize the main screen layout and features from other Joomla! backend manager screens. The **New** and **Edit** buttons allow you to enter URLs to be redirected and to change the URL details, the **Enable/Disable** buttons allow you to either activate or deactivate selected URL redirects, and you can send selected items to the **Archive** or to the **Trash**.

In the course of time, the **Expired URL** column in the **Redirect Manager: Links** screen will automatically be populated with broken links. These are URLs that visitors have entered or clicked on in their browser and that have generated an error page. Clicking on an expired URL will allow you to enter a redirect URL. However, if you've just installed Joomla! or if your site isn't live yet, the **Redirect Manager: Links** screen won't contain any Expired URLs.

2. Click on **New** to open the **Redirect Manager: Link** screen:

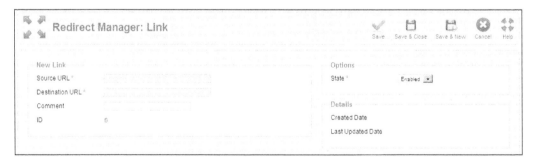

3. In the **Source URL** field, enter the outdated URL. Make sure to enter not just any wrong URL; it should contain the domain name from the current site. Replace **www.example.com** in the example below with your own domain name:

4. To determine the URL you want to redirect visitors to, navigate to the new page to copy the URL from the browser address field. To do this, click on **View Site** to open the website in a new browser tab. Navigate to the page you want to redirect visitors to. Don't copy the example URL below—navigate to an *existing page on your site:*

5. Copy the URL in the browser URL field using *Ctrl* + *C*. The URL data is now stored in the clipboard.

6. Click on the browser tab that takes you back to the backend of your site, displaying the **Redirect Manager: Link** screen again.

7. In the **Destination URL** field, paste the copied URL using *Ctrl* + *V*:

8. In the **Comment** field, you can enter a short note about the nature of this redirect—for example "redirecting from old About Us page".

9. You can leave the **Options** unchanged. Actually, there's just one option available: you can either enable or disable this redirect. The redirect is turned on by default, so that's OK.

10. Click on **Save & Close**. You're done. To test the redirect, navigate to the frontend of the site and enter the expired URL. You shouldn't get any error messages now; you're immediately taken to the new URL.

Redirecting multiple old URLs in one go

In the course of time, the Joomla! Redirect plugin may record a long list of expired URLs from pages that don't exist anymore—for example, different pages from a site category that you haven't taken along to your new site. As there are no new equivalent pages on your current site, you may want to redirect visitors to one new catch-all URL: a page explaining that you've restructured your blog and suggesting relevant links. Here's a quick way to redirect a group of outdated links to one new **Destination URL**:

1. In the **Redirect Manager: Links** screen, select all the URLs you want to point to the one new page you've created.

2. At the bottom of the screen, there's a section called **Update selected links to the following new URL**:

3. Enter the address of the new page in the **Destination URL** field and click on the **Update Links** button. The **Redirect Manager: Links** screen now displays the new URL in the **New URL** column of all the selected pages. All new redirect links are enabled.

4. That's it! You've now redirected a bunch of old URLs in one go. If you try any of the old pages on the frontend of your site, you're redirected to the new URL.

More on SEO

If you want to delve a little deeper into the principles of SEO for your website, make sure have a look at the Google starter guide on SEO (http://www.google.com/webmasters/docs/search-engine-optimization-starter-guide.pdf). In the Joomla! extensions directory, there's a growing number of valuable SEO extensions for Joomla! 1.6. See http://extensions.joomla.org/extensions/site-management/seo-a-metadata.

Summary

In this chapter, we've seen that Joomla! 1.6 takes some great steps forward in helping you create a site that should be able to be picked up and ranked well by search engines:

- The new semantic layouts are a big step forward towards a SEO-friendly site. Joomla! now outputs well-structured pages following current standards, which improves the search engine's ability to effectively index web page content.

- Use proper heading elements when writing and editing articles. Joomla! already uses H1 and H2 tags for the site title and page heading, so you should use only H3, H4, H5, and H6 headings in article text.

- If you want to manually control a specific HTML Page Title, you can set this in the Menu Item details.

- In Joomla! 1.6, you can enter metadata on four levels: site-wide, for individual menu links, for individual categories, and for individual articles.

- Search Engine Friendly URLs are now turned on by default.

- Joomla! 1.6 enables you to add a site map, using a new menu item type called **List All Categories**, but it's also possible to add a site map with more functionality using a dedicated site map extension.

- The new **Redirect Manager** can be quite useful, especially if you're migrating a Joomla! 1.5 site to 1.6. The Redirect Manager helps you to direct visitors from expired URLs to new URLs.

Index

C

categories
  about 13
  permissions for 121, 122
  settings 57
Category - Category Blog Layout 92
Category - Category List Layout 92
category contents
  displaying, on frontend 58
Category Manager 50
category metadata
  adding 57, 58
category structure
  displaying, on frontend 14
CCK 49
Clean Cache menu item 29
cleaner code
  about 161, 162
  need for 163
components
  permissions for 120, 121
configure, permission 121
content
  migrating, from Joomla! 1.5 9
  organizing, nested categories used 49-51
Content Construction Kit. *See* CCK
contentheading 162
content management system, Joomla! 1.6
  about 12
  categories 12-14
  menus 16
Copy button 88
create, permission 121, 122

D

default permissions 112
default site-wide settings 112, 113
default user groups
  about 112, 114
  admnistrator 115
  author 114
  customers 115
  editor 114
  manager 115

public, guest group 114
publisher 114
registered users 114
shop suppliers 115
super user 115
delete, permission 121, 122
Details section 91
Discover screen, Extension Manager 146
Display Options panel 98
DIV elements 162
dummy content
  creating, as Save as Copy button 37, 38

E

Edit Menu Item screen 91
  module settings, changing via 154-157
editors 114
edit own, permission 121, 122
edit, permission 121, 122
edit state, permission 121, 122
Empty Trash button 90
Expired Cache menu item 29
extension compatibility, Joomla! 1.5 8
Extension Manager
  about 143
  tabs 144-146
Extension Manager, tabs
  install 144
  manage 145
  update 144, 145
  warnings 146
extensions
  about 18, 139
  downloading, for Joomla! 1.6 158
  searching, for Joomla! 1.6 158

F

Flash image uploader
  enabling 73-75
frontend
  category contents, displaying on 58
  category structure, displaying on 14
Front Page - Front Page Blog Layout 92

G

Global Check-in menu item 29
Global Check-in option 30
global configuration
  site-wide permissions 118-120
Global Configuration | System screen 30

H

H1 page heading
  adding 189, 190
H3
  adding, through H6 headings 189
Hathor 43
hathor template 178
header image file
  changing 171
Home button 32
HTML5 177
HTML elements 187
HTML heading elements
  about 188, 189
  alternative H1 page heading, adding
    189-191
  H3, adding through H6 headings 189
  page heading and page title, differences
    191
HTML page titles
  configuring 192
  setting 192
  site name, adding 193, 194
hyperlink
  article title, inserting as 72, 73

I

index.php file 183
installed templates
  editing 176
  exploring 176
Install screen, Extension Manager 144
integration options, menu item options 102
item
  deleting 40, 41
  deleting, permanently 42

J

Joomfish 141
Joomla!
  about 23, 139
  modules, features 146
Joomla! 1.5
  content, migrating from 9
  extension compatibility 8
  upgrading from 7
Joomla! 1.6
  about 7, 23, 49, 139
  Access Control Levels 111
  ACL system 17, 18
  admin 25
  articles, archiving 75, 76
  Articles Categories module 63- 65
  Articles Category module 63-69
  backend, logging into 26, 27
  category listings, adding 65
  content management system 12-16
  Extension Manager 143-146
  extensions 18
  extensions, downloading for 158
  extensions, searching for 158
  HTML elements 187
  HTML heading elements 188, 189
  individual Menu Items 90, 91
  Media Manager 73
  Menu Manager screen 81, 82
  multi-language feature 141
  Note field 150, 151
  Redirect Manager 140, 203
  requisites 7
  root user 25
  root user's name, changing 25, 26
  search engine friendly URLs 198
  search engine, optimizing 20
  site map 200
  site metadata 194, 195
  super user 25
  tabbed Template Manager 164
  table-less templates 161, 162
  templates 8, 18, 19
  updated article editor 70, 71
  usability enhancements 10-12

Thank you for buying
Joomla! 1.6 First Look

About Packt Publishing

Packt, pronounced 'packed', published its first book "*Mastering phpMyAdmin for Effective MySQL Management*" in April 2004 and subsequently continued to specialize in publishing highly focused books on specific technologies and solutions.

Our books and publications share the experiences of your fellow IT professionals in adapting and customizing today's systems, applications, and frameworks. Our solution based books give you the knowledge and power to customize the software and technologies you're using to get the job done. Packt books are more specific and less general than the IT books you have seen in the past. Our unique business model allows us to bring you more focused information, giving you more of what you need to know, and less of what you don't.

Packt is a modern, yet unique publishing company, which focuses on producing quality, cutting-edge books for communities of developers, administrators, and newbies alike. For more information, please visit our website: www.packtpub.com.

About Packt Open Source

In 2010, Packt launched two new brands, Packt Open Source and Packt Enterprise, in order to continue its focus on specialization. This book is part of the Packt Open Source brand, home to books published on software built around Open Source licences, and offering information to anybody from advanced developers to budding web designers. The Open Source brand also runs Packt's Open Source Royalty Scheme, by which Packt gives a royalty to each Open Source project about whose software a book is sold.

Writing for Packt

We welcome all inquiries from people who are interested in authoring. Book proposals should be sent to author@packtpub.com. If your book idea is still at an early stage and you would like to discuss it first before writing a formal book proposal, contact us; one of our commissioning editors will get in touch with you.

We're not just looking for published authors; if you have strong technical skills but no writing experience, our experienced editors can help you develop a writing career, or simply get some additional reward for your expertise.

Joomla! 1.5: Beginner's Guide

ISBN: 978-1-847199-90-4   Paperback: 380 pages

Build and maintain impressive user-friendly web sites the fast and easy way with Joomla! 1.5

1. Create a web site that meets real-life requirements by following the creation of an example site with the help of easy-to-follow steps and ample screenshots

2. Practice all the Joomla! skills from organizing your content to completely changing the site's looks and feel

3. Go beyond a typical Joomla! site to make the site meet your specific needs

Building Websites with Joomla! 1.5

ISBN: 978-1-847195-30-2   Paperback: 384 pages

The best-selling Joomla! tutorial guide updated for the latest 1.5 release

1. Learn Joomla! 1.5 features

2. Install and customize Joomla! 1.5

3. Configure Joomla! administration

4. Create your own Joomla! templates

Please check **www.PacktPub.com** for information on our titles

Joomla! 1.5 Cookbook

ISBN: 978-1-84951-236-7   Paperback: 340 pages

Over 60 quick and direct recipes to help you overcome common Joomla! queries.

1. Find quick solutions to common Joomla! problems

2. Part of Packt's Cookbook series: Each recipe is a carefully organized sequence of instructions to complete the task as efficiently as possible

3. Look at recipes that cover the portions of Joomla! 1.6 that are brand new

4. Over 60 practical recipes covering a range of site management and core Joomla! activities

Joomla! 1.5 Development Cookbook

ISBN: 978-1-847198-14-3   Paperback: 360 pages

Solve real world Joomla! 1.5 development problems with over 130 simple but incredibly useful recipes

1. Simple but incredibly useful solutions to real world Joomla! 1.5 development problems

2. Rapidly extend the Joomla! core functionality to create new and exciting extension

3. Hands-on solutions that takes a practical approach to recipes - providing code samples that can easily be extracted.

Joomla! 1.5x Customization: Make Your Site Adapt to Your Needs

ISBN: 978-1-847195-16-6   Paperback: 288 pages

Create and customize a professional Joomla! site that suits your business requirements

1. Adapt your site to get a unique appearance, features, and benefits of your choice

2. Save on development costs by learning how to do professional work yourself and solve common problems with a Joomla! site

3. Step through how to build an effective subscription-based business with Joomla! and market a site effectively

Mastering Joomla! 1.5 Extension and Framework Development Second Edition

ISBN:978-1-849510-52-3   Paperback: 560 pages

Extend the power of Joomla! by adding components, modules, plugins, and other extensions

1. In-depth guide to programming Joomla! 1.5 Framework

2. Design and build secure and robust components, modules, and plugins

3. Customize the document properties, add multilingual capabilities, and provide an interactive user experience

Joomla! 1.5 Site Blueprints

ISBN: 978-1-849511-70-4   Paperback: 270 pages

Tailor-made plans for easily building powerful and exciting Joomla! sites

1. Instant Joomla! – Build 10 exciting and simple web projects

2. Expand and tailor the sample projects to your or your client's need

3. Create quick prototypes of commonly used applications within hours

4. Develop your own custom application by merging features from the example projects

Building job sites with Joomla!

ISBN: 978-1-84951-222-0   Paperback: 236 pages

A practical stepwise tutorial to build your professional website using Joomla!

1. Build your own monster.com using Joomla!

2. Take your job site to the next level using commercial Jobs! Extension

3. Administrate and publish your Joomla! job site easily using the Joomla! 1.5 administrator panel and Jobs! Pro control panel interface

4. Boost your job site ranking in search engines using Joomla! SEO

Please check **www.PacktPub.com** for information on our titles

www.ingramcontent.com/pod-product-compliance
Lightning Source LLC
Chambersburg PA
CBHW080404060326
40689CB00019B/4127